Ruth Sharman
Alison Spritzler-Rose
Catherine Conzato
John Gower

TWO + TWO

Staple
FIRST EDITION
1997

T W O + T W O

Staple First Editions

ISBN 0 9510523 9 X

TYPESET
by
ROGER BOOTH ASSOCIATES
HASSOCKS, WEST SUSSEX
IN NEW BASKERVILLE

PRINTED
at
THE ARC & THROSTLE PRESS
NANHOLME MILL, TODMORDEN

DESIGN
by
BILL AND LUCY BERRETT

PUBLISHED
by
Staple NEW WRITING
15 JULY 1997

Staple
is published with
financial assistance
from East Midlands
Arts

CONTENTS

Ruth Sharman

Alison Spritzler-Rose

RUTH SHARMAN

KNIFE
and other poems

For my mother and father

RUTH SHARMAN

Dominic Turner

Ruth Sharman was born in Madras and came to live in England at the age of six. She read Modern Languages at Cambridge, where she was awarded a PhD for an edition of the poetry of a 12th-century troubadour, Giraut de Borneil. She won second prize in the Arvon International Poetry Competition in 1989 and was runner-up in the National the following year, and has had poems published in a number of magazines and national newspapers. She currently works in London as a freelance translator. Her first collection, *Birth of the Owl Butterflies*, is due from Picador in November.

TOUCH

That was the garden where I'd ride horses
whose names I'd heard on TV
and written in my private book,
and where I planted London Pride and trimmed
a two-foot square of lawn with bathroom scissors.

From the plum tree I could see the sky
and look across the fields that rolled up
to our garden fence and down to where
a curve of trees followed the contours
of the hills and hid a stream

I'd spend hours damming and undamming,
where only water sounds would break
the stillness or a sudden flash
of wings, and in spring a mass of violets
flowered in the shadows, scented, white.

There were three of us building dams
the day the big boys came and told us
to take off our clothes and *Touch. Go on, touch,*
so we shackled our knees with trouser legs
and touched each other in places
                    we'd not touched before.

They laughed, kicked a stone or two and left...
We watched as water seeped at first,
then prised apart all that our hands had done
and the whole muddy torrent came bursting through
with its cargo of leaves and scum.

FIRST SNOW

Flame trees flowered
around the garden walls –
flames before the leaves –

and on the pond
waterlilies opened,
crimson, after dark

and on nights too hot
for pillows we'd swim
under the Gymkhana lights

eat chips in chilli sauce
and sleep on the roof
to catch the breeze.

And even if poisonous
red centipedes lived
inside the potting shed

October winds tore down
the trees and a cobra
took my white dove, even if

people who had no hands
and only half a face
came begging at the gate

these were things I knew
and nothing whitened
that first sky.

At five I left behind
one mother who'd held me
through the monsoon nights

and sailed across an ocean
with the other to a place
of washed-out skies

where there were clocks,
School, shoelaces and ties,
a whole new way of eating

a garden full of nettles,
a house whose roof of straw
let in the rain

and the day I woke
to a whiteness that stole
the shadows from the trees

rubbed out colours
and stopped the sounds
it was then I knew for sure

the world I knew had died.

THE THING

My father got it wrong
the day he caught me kissing
by the garden gate
and raged and said
(if not in terms)
his daughter was a whore.

Kisses were okay
but I shrank
from the something more
boys seemed to want
and can't forget the shock
that time one stuffed

my hand inside his flies
and I touched hair
where I'd expected skin
and felt that thing
rise up and lumber
from its clammy lair.

RUTH

I envy her
as she stoops
from dawn till dusk

day after day
as the wheat is reaped,
and the barley

rubbing her fingers raw
in the dust
and the heat.

I envy her
dipping her bread
in the strangers' bowl

sipping their water,
avoiding
their eyes.

I envy her
going to lie each night
in her narrow bed

widow-daughter
who when her mother-in-law
said she must

laid herself
at the man's feet,
offering herself like a whore.

I envy her,
afraid no well of mine
is deep enough

and those I love
must drink elsewhere.

YELLOW

It's the colour of crocuses
clamouring for the sun

like a nestful
of blackbird beaks

the colour of pussy willow
pollen-furred

lemons and pudding wine
a last freckling of leaves

lightening the darkness
of sycamore trees

of paper spotted by time
and milk gone sour

something leaked
on to hospital white

and my mother's face
on her hospital pillow

small and tight
and beaked like a bird's.

MORPHINE

Nothing could prepare us for this.

After plumped pillows
and talk of Christmas.
You wearing that white shawl
from Kashmir,
saying what bulbs to plant
for the spring.

You now
like this

baby bird
at the bottom of a tree,
head on one side,
flesh stretched taut
over tiny bones

brown blotches seeping across your skin
like blotting stains

so small I could almost lift you
out of the bed

so small I might snap
your arms.

Nothing could prepare me

for the way you whiten
and harden

and how it feels
to wrench the rings
from your fingers.

WORDS

My mother had trouble with words.
I doubt she'd have known 'metastasise'
until her illness spilled and spread:
a tongue-twister to add to her confusion.
Flustered by clever company she'd mispronounce
the easiest ones; forget, say, the soft g
in rouge, and later glow with shame.

Hers was a vocabulary of growing things.
Hooped petticoats and peeping Toms
were daffodils she loved for their dainty names
and even Latin came easily when applied
to those lilies of the haziest blue
or the shrub that blazed by the garden wall
and needed shielding from the frost.

She preferred a wilderness to a park,
encouraging leaves to spill, coaxing
our tiny garden to year-round disarray.
And when a cool oasis greened between
our limestone walls, took refuge in its shade:
protecting her complexion from carcinomas
that budded deep inside her when they came.

OUT THERE

This was you in the early days
wearing that wide blue skirt
and your camera smile,
cream-skinned despite the heat.

You'd sailed the length of Suez.
Seen shoals of silver fish in flight
and the flame trees' leafless
branches catching light.

You'd crossed Himalayan passes
among iris and poppy fields,
picnicked on white beaches
and summered in the hills;

worn marigold garlands, fingered
fruit shaped like hearts and stars
while lepers groped for handouts
and small birds sang behind bars.

You'd learnt to kill your time
taking tea at the Gymkhana pool
and later cocktails, relinquishing
your children to the rules;

letting others fix the backdrop
of your day: sweep the paths,
make the beds, mop our faces,
cook the meals, drive the cars.

And already forty years ago
you had that frown around your eyes
as you looked back past the camera
to another life, one more your size.

BIRTH OF THE OWL BUTTERFLIES

They hung in our kitchen for days.
A row of brown lanterns that threw no light,
merely darkened with their growing load.
Pinned to a shelf among the knick-knacks
and the cookery books;
ripening in the radiator's heat:
six Central American *Caligo* chrysalises
five thousand miles from their mountain home.

My father had brought them here,
carefully packed in cotton wool,
to hatch, set, identify, and display:
these unpromising dingy shells plumped up
like curled leaves, on each a tiny gleam,
a silver spur, or drop of dew,
Nature had added as a finishing touch
to perfect mimicry.

For weeks the wizened fruit had been maturing.
Now, one by one, the pods exploded,
crackling loudly in the quiet kitchen,
and a furry missile emerged
– rapid, as if desperate to break free –
unhinged its awkward legs,
hauling behind it, like a frilly party dress,
the rumpled mass of its soft wings.

It clung unsteadily to the cloven pod,
while slow wings billowed with the blood
that pumped them full.
The dark velvet began to glow
with a thousand tiny striations,
and there, in each corner,
boldly ringed in black and gold,
two fierce owl eyes widened.

Uneasy minutes before *Caligo*
can flex its nine-inch wings and fly.
They drooped still, gathering strength,
limp flags loosely flowing.
When two butterflies hatched too close,
and clashed, each scrabbling for a footing,
one fell and its wings flopped
fatly against the kitchen floor.

I pictured them shattering later
on taps and cupboard corners;
but my father gauged his moment well,
allowed a first few timid forays,
then swooped down gentle-fingered
with his glass jar for the kill.
The monstrous wings all but filled it,
beat vigorously, fluttered, and were still.

MAKING JAM

It was magic of a sort, the way
she let the drops of syrup fall, to form
those solid jewels on her setting plate
while night closed in around the kitchen's warmth.

The ripe fruit spread its sweetness through the house
and as she stirred, the purple darkness turned
to deepest rose that seethed and frothed, white, round
the edges of her pan, and slowly firmed.

She'd make as much as twenty pots at once
in better years. We find the odd one still
tucked in behind the packet soups and tins
on shelves that home-made things of hers once filled.

And as the written labels slowly blur,
her elixir now grows a soft white fur.

'FOR JOY ...'

I have a store of names
that make me think of you:
Grayling, Gatekeeper,
Comma, Ringlet, Marbled White
and Meadow Brown,
the Queen of Spain
and all her English relatives ...

reminding me of all the times
I've followed you
through some wilderness
of wood or marsh or scrub,
the hours (it seemed) I'd sit
and wait while you went on,
and then complain.

And now I'm adding to the list
as I watch with you
for orange flashes
in the wind:
we scramble up a ferny combe
looking down to Porlock
and to Wales across the water

and when I ask you why
a Fritillary
with just three weeks to fly
should choose this windy hillside
high above the sea,
your answer makes me glad
to be my father's daughter.

ILLUSTRATIONS OF THE BRITISH FLORA

My father bought me this sober little book
when I was still too young to comprehend
the reproductive processes in flowers,
its references to ovules, perianths and angiosperms.

The plates showed in black and white a hundred
varieties of grass and puzzled us with *Compositae*
and Umbellifers that were hard to tell apart,
encouraging a 'Spot the Difference' of our own.

After each walk I'd colour in another vetch or daisy,
blurring the edges like an old lady's lipstick,
adding 'Nobottle Woods' or 'marsh' or 'disused railway'
in writing that joined up with the years.

The book was my bible, symbol of a private dialogue
with my dad (who always did talk best through things)
and as I look at the crinkled creamy pages,
at all the blank spaces among the brightness

I want to see those missing flowers filled in
and write the names for places we never knew
until each page is thick with ink and pastel
and all that was left unsaid is said in silence now.

THE ISLAND
(after Arnold Böcklin)

What most attracts our eye
is not the sheer rock rising
out of black water

not the caverns carved in the cliffs,
the black cypress trees,
the bruised end-of-evening sky

but this woman dressed in white
drifting towards an entrance
beneath the trees

towards a flight of steps, a door,
some opening up of space
we sense but cannot see

and we long for the boat to land,
for the frozen figure to alight
and climb the stairs

and we wonder what the darkness
can reveal but walls of rock
and empty rooms.

WOMAN DRYING HERSELF
(after Degas)

Her back is curved like a leaf
on one of those poplars
he wouldn't paint,

moving freely in the wind,
catching light as it turns,
holding firmly to a stem

so strong and supple, you'd say
in other lives she might have bent
to lift potatoes from the soil

or forked in hay, whitened sheets,
ironed and folded, and walked
with children on her hips.

Where it dips to meet her spine
like hills down to a cleave
he gave her the colour

of sweetbriers and gorse stalks
charred by summer fires,
while light from an unseen source

has opalised her shoulderblade
and thigh, the curving
river of her arm.

One orange slipper, a hint of
auburn hair, and a hundred years on
she breathes and burns,

while the man who made her
shunned the sunlight
because it hurt his bloodshot eyes.

CONGER

We watch him.
Lying there bloated and still
in the shadows.
Blue-black fruit
that's ready to burst.

I wonder
if I dipped my finger in,
would he lunge,
though he's already breakfasted
on dead flesh?

If I wrapped my hands
round his waist
– though they'd never reach –
would he feel like warm velvet
or cold and slick like slime?

Since he's no more
than an eating machine,
would I even know
where his belly began?

We watch
for a flicker of life
from lightless eyes.
            Then suddenly
this eel that's she to you
and he to me
shifts like a shadow
beyond our grasp.

KNIFE

Some vegetables
resist more vigorously
than others.

To vary things
she plays at cutting
herringbones and ovals,

teasing the skin
with her point before
penetrating the heart,

pictures a fingertip
nestling among peelings
on the spattered board,

and, for the luxury
of granting him
a reprieve perhaps,

imagines stepping
to where her husband sits
absorbed

and steering the knife
quite casually
into his side,

curious to see
his look of surprise, feel
how smoothly a blade can slide.

MUMMY

Dearest, we'll start by removing
the bits you won't need any more

– just a delicate cut,
before bathing you inside and out –

then we'll sweeten your flesh
with cinnamon, cedar and myrrh.

So you shine like a god, we'll wrap leaves
of electrum round fingers and toes,

and those muscular shoulders and legs
we'll keep toned

by secreting soft shavings of *Ficus*
just under the skin.

We'll salt you in crystals of natron
and bathe you again.

Then we'll bind. Do it finger
by finger,

and strap down those hands that have strayed,
in a cross at your heart.

With your torso and limbs we'll arrange
a neat parcel in lattice designs

while reserving the narrowest bands
for your head,

which we'll wrap from the left,
then the right, the same number of times,

gently sealing those lips that have lied
with the linen's soft kiss.

Once you're upright, I'll breathe
in your mouth

and I'll open your eyes
to a world in which nothing has changed.

All around will be things that you know.
You'll have garlands and honey with milk

while that niche by the door
will be perfectly placed

for watching me come
and then go.

THE BRIDE

They always told me I was bad,
so it was a shock
to hear my dad talking
about his lovely daughter
(the lovely child she'd always been).
It was no good though
– too late to hear such praise –
and as he spoke
I put aside my lilies
and unpinned the veil
that floated down my tight-laced back,
then one by one uncoiled
each strand of hair
from the heavy mass around my head.
My father raised his glass.
The guests picked up their own,
and as they gazed at me
what they saw were hissing snakes
and what I saw was stone.

THE DRESS

I wandered through a mansion in my dream
where countless dresses hung from countless rails.
Some were made of velvet, some of silk,
chenille or lace, and some were filmy veils
that slipped beneath my fingertips, soft
and shimmering in shades of white and cream.

I chose one and my husband helped me in.
In cut and shape it differed from the rest,
tapering to a mermaid's tail, its neck
revealing curves I lacked in life.
                              The dress
he hooked me into was my wedding dress,
and it was black and fitted like a skin.

BAD GIRL

He only hits her
when she asks for it.
Only when she dresses
a certain way
and confesses
she's been bad.

He wants her
to want this pain

and it's not with pain
that she cries
but knowing
she'll do it again
and again and not know
who for, or why.

26

ALISON SPRITZLER-ROSE

SEVENTEEN POEMS

ALISON SPRITZLER-ROSE

Quintin Wright

Alison Spritzler-Rose lives in London where she writes a regular column for The Erotic Print Society Review. She has been placed in numerous poetry competitions including the Bridport Prize, Ver Poets Prize, the Kensington & Chelsea Arts Council Prize and, most recently, fifth place in the 1997 Peterloo Poets Competition. An illustrated pamphlet, *Cow, Cherries & Fish People*, is published by Clarion Press in the Prospero Poets Series. Her poems have appeared in *The Observer* and a short story in *The Printer's Devil*. She has written lyrics for Momus and for Chester Kamen, poetry reviews for the *TLS* and book reviews for the *Catholic Herald*. Currently she is editing her first novel.

DOROTHY

This is everything you always wanted to know
about strangers:

This is a man mistaking you for someone else.
You reply, I am.

This is the next eight hours which pass
like scenery from a train you're not on.

This is six day-glow vodka jellies later –
your party was another two doors down.

We're not in Kansas, anymore.

This is where you stagger from the minicab
and force your keys into someone else's door.

This is 4am, you, or someone who looks like you
hollering to be let in.

Dorothy, this is your street-lamp soliloquy,
as you audition for the role of your self
and pray you get the part.

PENELOPE

Taking turns on the table top
my sister pinstriped cool black eye-liner
from my ankles to an inch above my hem.
    Hold still.

1944, her man returned – a prize scar
snaking across his abdomen. Mine hasn't yet.
I once cracked a rib, laughing over nothing.
    It never healed.

Now each night Joy's Dance Hall
meets the wrecker's ball.
A million shrapnel lights
    tilt the sprung floor.

Swirling toss and turn, I wake
to find the backs of my legs flayed
and then I stitch them back together
    at the seams.

JOSEPHINE

Mon très cher,

the empire's silhouette
is like your cloak across the planet.
The rest, four fifths water
and all the fish in the sea

inhabit none of this
as you inhabit me.

You are so far from these sweet gardens,
where I breakfast on the darkest plums.
I forget the musket of the battlefield

that draws the blood
that sets the seal,

and of how black tenderness can seem
when I read in your sweet hand
'My cruellest Josephine'.

PACIFIC

Let's jump the broom, the young man said.
Next spring they were married in a vineyard,
an entire sun-specked village for witness.
Or there's a quick Las Vegas, gracing
the pink-lit pavilion in Stetson and mini.
There's the flip-side, the other country:
I divorce thee, I divorce thee, I divorce thee.

Meanwhile, things go missing: your initials
from the monogram, now looking like Sanskrit.
The list that reads like a robbery, when possessions
turn, decide to own you; the way the gate
keeps calling you back to check that it's locked;
the wide gravel drive that fails its destination,
that can't stop rising and falling.

The land's sea-sawing cut-out through the portal
of a ship. Port outward, starboard home. Or the
other way around. Name your position.
All of it passing and nearly gone:
the way you let his hand touch yours,
without touching, forgetting your umbrella,
knowing you 'haven't the sense to come in

from the rain' – as if water could harm you.
But there's weight in oceans. A liner takes miles
to turn. There's the hard creak of the iceberg,
starting in the garden, pushing
its moon face to freeze the kitchen window,
convexing the bedroom wall that is even now
heaving with a snore.

CHERRIES

Being terribly bored I have decided
to give a cocktail party.
I will be wearing pigtails.
You may wear what you wish.

Life is a bowl of cherries.
My mother has a special syringe
for ejecting the pips.

It's non-stop sunshine
for the scriptwriters and blondes
who sunbathe between palms
and slender bamboo.

I seem to live permanently
in a yellow lace party dress
and shiny red-buckle shoes.

Today I rode my tricycle
straight into the swimming pool.
Ejected from the tasseled handle-bars
I sank like a stone.
Two red shoes floated to the surface.

EMPIRE STATE

The day your girlfriend kicked you out
you wandered around New York City
for sixteen hours,
managed to get yourself mugged
out of guilt
and rang me at 8am from the top
of the Empire State.
Go on the roof, you said –
Wear white and wave your arms.

I imagined you microscopic at the other end
of a nickel telescope.
If you waved back
my eyes were too small by then to see it.

ISLAND

While the traction of polished gears
let drop the iron counter-balance,
we rose, pulling gravity with us.
Alone at last in the soundproof glass lift,

we found the only safe place for a kiss.

But as we watched the lobby recede
its fountain looked like the blow-hole
of the great leviathan, which those sailors,
dropping anchor, mistook for an island.

CAKE

When an item (for item read atrocity)
was censored, they inserted a recipe instead –
usually lemon cheesecake.

On pain of death I could not now
tell you those ingredients.
Perhaps I should leave an eloquent gap
in this text:

6 sponge fingers
dash essence of ammonia
2 cups boiling water
a lemon for your wounds.

THE BUNGEE JUMPERS

When the tightrope leads nowhere, precariously –
let us knot the thing into a harness,
its cross at our back. Forget the art
of the trapeze; we're aching to fall, not fly.

Thrill-seekers of the great blue toy, death's
just a figure of speech, something to queue for,
to do again and again – Here we are, toes upturned,
risking it all for the sign of a pulse.

We used to swing through trees – no safety catch
no trick behind the scenes, no rubberised umbilical lead,
no world attached to its other end.
Look at us now –

Rigged up for the trip like a bored Icarus
here for the suntan, hardly getting our noses wet.

OPTIQUE

The sun hovers like God's one eye, open
to fix mankind in its pain.

And I too, in this kingdom of the blind,
shut tight one eye when I take aim.

TARGET PRACTICE

After I killed the petrol attendant
(while she read the Sun on the front seat)
I propped the bugger up like a straw Guy
and hopped back in, the job complete.

You've no idea the beauty of sunset –
that slow catastrophe of reds and golds.
Myself, I'm still waiting for the flip-side,
moonset. The final curtain to this show.

These frigging nights and days just never end.
TV makes my head hum, sex just jars it.
So tonight I'm teaching her to load, draw,
aim – to fit a silencer. Muzzle, click.

We climb to the roof for target practice.
I love her arms, rigid as a verdict.
Then I whisper to the down of her neck
'Hit the moon. Try to sink it.'

HELSINKI

We're watching TV, or the TV's glow.
The evening forecast ought to be simple.
'Low C will drift north and deepen.
High tides. Cold front from Helsinki.'
I don't know what an isobar is
nor where this crack in your wall leads.
I think you were born knowing all these things.

We don't go out because it's cold.
We eat pistachios in bed,
spilling the shells into the sheets.
I set aside the fistful that won't open.
Later I dream we're in Helsinki.
I'm running with a sharp pebble in my shoe.
You're shouting over your shoulder, 'Hurry!'

ANATOMY

Remember when they dressed piano legs in skirts
because a bit of wood on a castor
could thrill?

When you rested your leg on the desk,
with everyone else too preoccupied to notice,
I witnessed a vulnerable malleolus.

I know I shouldn't think these thoughts –
the way your trouser leg rides up,
and you in no socks.

I imagine the crook behind the patella,
warm tendons to pluck
and between each,
the pale hollows of flesh –
such tenderness.

VOODOO

or acupuncture
or just plain tactics –

I was your map of Africa –
your heart of darkness,

your Poland –
that *piece of cake*,

your strategy for a policy
of pinpricks
which ends in bleeding one
to death.

I was your harpooned whale,
your honeyed porcupine,
your saint of all Sebastians.

VISITING RIGHTS

We'll visit the Museum of Forgotten Things
where we'll see The Vase That Was Never Broken
and watch the demonstration
of what birthday presents look like
before they are opened.

We'll stop for ice cream.
You'll order vanilla in a cup.
On the way back we'll pass the man
with the blind dog.
We'll ask that dog's name for once
and remember it.

We'll start on a Sunday
going backwards through the week
pretending none of this
ever happened.

HOME MOVIES

Last night I dreamed you were alive again.
We were sitting on that aromatic cow-hide couch
watching the screen.

You cleared your throat and leaned forward
to tap your pipe on the ashtray's edge
and I reminded myself by passing my hand
through you, that you were dead.

I watched you all night, sitting with a blank stare
as you watched my life pass before you,
like a film but in real time. I heard my own voice
when I was a child of nine:

I am pouring lemonade. 'Is that enough?'
By dawn the screen grows faint.
I switch it off and hear the last word echo –
'enough, enough, enough'.

My image fades to a dot
but you continued to watch the space
where we once existed.
I sat beside you and held your unborn hand.
I stayed beside you all night long.

CONSTELLATION

Snapped twig –
seven shadow rabbits
halt
at my approach.

The white undersides
of their tails
flash
like fire beacons.

I navigate
a nervous constellation
that guides me
in all directions.

CORK

Mis en Bouteille au Domaine
is all this lavender-tipped note says.

I know you only drink alone
when Ireland is a long way away.

I will take a match to it,
write you a message in ash.

Let its name be its address.
Let its message be as true

as its journey,
weightless.

CATHERINE CONZATO

GORGEOUS EYES
and other stories

For Jenni

CATHERINE CONZATO

Francis Provençal

Catherine Conzato grew up in Sydney, Australia. She studied Modern African and Asian History at Sydney University before moving to Paris, where she worked as an au pair for a theatrical family and studied French. She moved to Milan to learn Italian, taught English to schoolchildren and bank employees, and translated welding manuals. She left Europe for Africa, spending two years working with the European Union Delegation in Mogadishu before civil war destroyed the city. After brief spells in Veneto and Brussels she moved to Ghana, where she has lived with her husband and three young children for the past four years. She writes full time at present and is an avid collector of West African art. Her stories have been published in Australian, English and US reviews and anthologies.

THE EGG RUN

There was a fragile aspect to her work that she had not yet explored. Then one Sunday morning that door was opened. Harriet called, oddly, in a raw voice trailing with both of their hampered desires. She was belligerent.

'You were asleep I suppose?'

Light crossed through the shutters. Broken and fumy like craft.

'Of course.'

'And the devil's in your bed?'

Kerri glanced beside her. She hated Harriet's assumption that they had twin failures.

'No, he's not. Not yet.'

Harriet paused. Kerri pictured Harriet's generous, loose form on the sheets, finetuning the gist of her silence. She waited.

'You've been to Winneba, haven't you?' Harriet continued.

'Yes.'

'Yeah, well a guy's drowned. It just happened now. They radioed.'

Kerri sat up, seeing flints on the wall suddenly, feeling prickly.

'There's no body,' Harriet went on. 'But they'll find it. You're bringing it to town for the autopsy. It's the law here before it gets sent back home.'

Kerri stirred. There was a clause in her contract dealing with Death. It hadn't halted her. The words were clear, naked, honest. Now she fretted, clinging to Harriet's voice but repelled by its content.

'I've got the parents' number. Though it's always best to call afterward. When everything's been verified. He was a volunteer on the schools' project. Down from the bush. Probably had a drink too many.'

Kerri took down the number, realising that it belonged to the suburb where she had passed most of her life. The frieze of her city came to mind, the antithesis of West Africa's steamy, stricken continuum where she was marooned now. She and the dead man might have lived in nearby streets, or passed in traffic queues. She damned the fact that they were linked.

'Take your van, not mine –' Harriet was saying now. Was it possible she was searching for kinder tones after her jealous heavy-handedness? 'And Jones if you want a driver. No, do take him, you might need help. Get a move on. It's a hot sun out there already –'

And it was true. As Harriet's voice dropped away Kerri felt the midmorning in full flush beyond her shutters. Palm leaves clattered, their trunks toiling in minute and grandiose ascension.

Birds squawked with early morning confidence; Ishmail's hose water slopped around her ferns.

What had happened here last night? Another blundered chapter in her absurd love life? It might have helped to tell Harriet yet another hopeful lie. But what the hell – Harriet had her own way of measuring your size, your gumption, your crude value. On their first expedition way, way up north to Bolgatanga, Harriet had crouched beside the stationary vehicle to pee. The earth was red and detailless. Harriet's trickle ran into the dust like a bitch marking out territory. Challenged – and needing to relieve herself – Kerri could only crouch beside her. From the start Kerri assumed their sisterhood would count more than the other ties she would forge in Ghana. And hadn't she been right? Who had there been? A Canadian dance student, a Spanish boy who vanished in love, Deirdre before she caught typhoid and, of late, the possibility of Marco. Kerri breathed again, soaking up the change of current now within the room. Where before it had worn the apparel of her almost-tryst, now it was the site where she'd lain in damp, ignorant sleep while some man she had to fetch was in the throes of drowning.

Briefly she sketched the beach. It was a long friendless stretch of sand beyond the town of Winneba. The coconut trees, victim of some disease, had half of them lost their tops and thus all semblance to earthly flora. They looked foreboding, their peculiar limbs at odds with the planet. It wasn't inappropriate for Death at all, she thought. That pulling tide, the trembling ire of the consumed man. It was a hazardous ocean. The way it carved the sandbed, the way it churned over only metres beyond the edge but sucked down carefully, cogently, to its depths of tawny shell crusts. Fishermen lost their lives regularly. Local kids were swept out; easy prey. Kerri felt the nastiness of her opponent.

What had happened there last night? Had there been a drinking party on the sand till late – members sure-handed in violet coves, their lovemaking barely fretted by sandbugs and the whining certitude of malaria? How was he? Freckled, tall, abusive? Or slower, even graceful, reluctant? Again her thought veered back to Marco. She knew so little, supposed so much. That they had worked together in an isolated hilltop town in the west had lacquered Harriet's comments with nuance. But Marco had the gentle, isolated ways of a man cradled by his own language. His harmony deranged her; he had overlooked her savouring of him. To Harriet, Kerri had lied impulsively about sparks flying, about the jugs of sweat. And thereafter smarted with it.

Only last night her and Marco's incongruence had appeared complete. He was here, in this very room, contemplating terrific silver and amber beads of hers in a leather box. He went on studiously while she sipped tea on a battered cane chaise-longue. That was their picture.

She leapt out of bed registering the digital clock, undressing by the time she reached the shower. In a minute she was out again, fastening a stringy bra, pulling on her gung-ho jeans with fastidious but useful thigh pockets. She pulled out a mascara tube but then replaced it, saddened. You didn't wear make-up on a death mission. She tied up her boots, packed her radio for her mid-morning report to Harriet. On her way out she snatched up a packet of flaky local biscuits.

Kerri's deepening aloneness had encouraged her to believe that all union was false, temporary and, if not, corrosive. When ill, her forces rallied against the virus, or malaria, or her own frequent exhaustion. She could feel a type of chemical turnaround each time she passed from sheer weakness to tottery defeat. In torment, she would be vexed until she reached this moment, and understood that her life was a simple swing between these two points. At thirty-six she was still hardy enough to follow this vicious pendulum, though in truth, she possessed no other lifeplan on which to peg her being.

Harriet called again, just once, as she was charging out of the driveway. Kerri was a reckless driver and had hit a young boy in the past. It was mown into her memory, the thrump of bones on metal. It wasn't her fault – the figure had been pitched at her by the dark. Kerri realised Harriet's voice had shot down to a different timbre.

'Okay, the body's been found. His girlfriend just called again. It's not going to be very pleasant. Jones is at the roundabout. You should reach Winneba in an hour or so. Bring it back to the clinic for the autopsy. I'll be waiting for you.'

In the meantime, then, Harriet must have sent one of her neighbour's kids out to Medina where Jones had a shack: had him roused and brushed down and brought in. Impressive. Did Kerri smell a favour?

'Are you there? Can you quit crunching those gears Kerri? It's a project vehicle and not your own damned bomb –'

'Yeah, right,' Kerri drawled.

Harriet came from the country and had shouldered her way into the organisation without a degree. Her father was a fairly odious personage on the rim of national politics, whom cartoonists regularly caricatured to high heaven. Other people had told Kerri that Harriet had failed everything else and landed here. Harriet hid her origins, but still expected an abominable amount of kow-towing. She got into rows with weedy devastated vets, student teachers were bewildered by her. Kerri was the one some of them came to afterward, bruised and vengeful:

'That bitch won't last long out here';

'I hope the locals roast her';

'Couldn't we splice her soda with bilharzia?'

Harriet spat into the receiver even louder. 'Kerri? Are you listening? I said Jones is at the roundabout. If you don't get your foot off the floor you'll miss him. Over.'

And yet Harriet must have learnt she was the nodule of the master plan. For all her aggravation, her crumbling insecurities, her sordid inference, she was a clean, effective worker. She thinned out funds and saw that their money flexed its muscle. The crudest school shed, the tackiest toilet block painted acid green, the most hopeless marketplace – she saw that they were all objects of solemn ceremony, respected and patronised, maintained by dogged parties she sent roaming the countryside on Pepsi and *banku*. She praised the locals for their frugality. Slammed people like Kerri because they attended cocktails, wore gold chains under their rusted shirts, carried on like the creamy Westerners they remained.

What did that make Harriet?

Kerri had visited Harriet's den and found it was strangely chaste, peculiarly holy. There were sofas surrounding a streaky chest, novels in a cane wall unit, the television enshrined by a caul of empty space. Harriet had been gravely ill in one instance. It had almost been a disaster. Even the Indian doctor had driven away, such that Kerri feared the stony force of his exit.

Rumours about Harriet thrived. The younger, hungrier members of staff were quick to plot against her. In spates she was a horny lesbian, a sick transvestite, or a beach prowler who paid for virulent sex. The sightings were pinned up. Kerri heard the older woman pickled, jabbed at, voodoo-ed. It was too easy to picture her lax form in connivance with a black Adonis, the slip of paper with an address, the young man's bravado and avid dress as he trod onto her patio, becalmed.

'And what of your boss? That disagreeable woman, Signora Mollar?' Even Kerri's almost-lover Marco had enquired, for these were the waves she had driven forth.

'Oh, Harriet,' Kerri had replied, irritated. 'Harriet's just big. She needs her moat. She's worried the space will cave in around her.'

He'd laughed soberly, not understanding a whit of what she'd said.

Kerri saw Jones on the knoll in the middle of the roundabout. It was his little stab at power reversal, given she sat there revving the engine while he sauntered forth. Jones was Harriet's driver. He had woven a quarter-century career between various Western aid groups. He had driven dignitaries, bought them sweaty cola from road bars, watched their insides fail them after capricious local meals. Jones reached the driver's side as she buzzed down the window, now able to hear the whip of the Togolese flag over the bedraggled embassy. His gappy smile suddenly opened on her.

'Morning Miss Toomey.'

'It's Kerri, Jones. Don't make me remind you on a Sunday.'

'Fine, Madame.'

'Oh come on, Jones! Hop in and take over. The big lady doesn't want me playing with her gears.'

Jones took the driver's seat and began his slowish, assured driving. Kerri stretched her legs, got out an empty dossier sheet and transferred her scribble to the official page. The drowned man had a name now: Leo Farquhar, aged 24. He had a phone number and an address – a busy, atrociously normal street Kerri had driven down aeons of times. She pictured some of the houses – their false awnings, their replaced window frames and incomplete gardens. They were houses where efforts had been made, then had fallen off.

She hated the flavour of mourning.

Outside the streetlife ran on, strangely muted beyond the vehicle's window frets. A boy's neck jerked under the weight of gathered sticks on his head. Women dragged fussily dressed girls, babies cocooned on their backs. Taxis chugged about, their drivers with woolly recollections of last night's palm wine. Young women rubbed raw went about the business of knowing what to forget.

Kerri doodled. The name Leo Farquhar meant nothing to her. And yet she must have met him. All of the young ones came to her at some stage – when their briefings were frayed, when they needed medicine, when their landlords squeezed too hard. Or when their programmes backfired and Harriet was too snarling to be approached. She was careful not to befriend them. Most thought that she was on Harriet's side initially and looked around for other props. At barbecues she made a point of securing the trust of two or three of them: inserting herself in their ground-sweeping arguments, tying a swift knot here and there, offering the contract of her eyes. She wasn't fishing for friendship, she found it made for easier work in the long run. Harriet said she was foolish for it – that one day she would put a foot wrong; that in the end you had to jettison everybody anyway. Kerri sighed and put the can on Harriet. Was it possible that Harriet had someone in bed herself this morning? A young beauty with bold thighs and muscles sketched over his abdomen?

She turned to Jones' blue-black profile. He had a large chin fraught with open pores, held prominently as he drove. Finding him suddenly indignant, Kerri made out she was following a kid skating along in the background, and then the crisscrossed iron bridge that lunged over and above them. She hadn't brought a flask of water, she remembered; she hadn't even eaten the crumbly biscuits she'd shoved in her pocket. She sat there.

The van moved through the city's edge. Harassed vehicles gathered at corners, or angrily along the single strip where the asphalt had been gulped away. Prominent, pretentious Macarthy Hill stood over the last Western-clad service stations, decked in houses of undressed brick. White bread sat on dirty benches. Bags of salt waited on tables between bitter trees. The salt plant stood there, a fixture of pastel walls with a humped, corrugated roof. The road bled past it into an ugly plain, over coarse hills.

Before the turn-off to the Westerners' beach a cropped Suzuki overtook them. It was Marco's jeep. Instantly Kerri's bones locked; liquids inside her began to race. As he passed them his profile tightened with risk: his was a fast, Italian manoeuvre. He slipped back into their lane before an oncoming *trotro*, accelerating away with now relaxed, unburdened shoulders.

Why had he not saluted her? Why, when it was so obvious from behind that Jones was driving her, and that this was her vehicle? Kerri re-examined their fruitless intimacy. They had eaten and drunk together, but it had not flowered. Had she been trying too hard to launch the moment they would collide? Or was it simpler? Was he gay or attached? But hell – she was not unattractive. She was thin, but she had good bones with taut, clear skin. Her face was not exceptional, but not bad either. Why had she fallen upon an Italian with principles? And not one who would just roll her hurtfully, but surely that would hurt less?

As Jones too accelerated – possibly to show this white man a portion of his stuff – Kerri recognised the t-shirt Marco was wearing. Stencilled on the front was some temple or palace encircled by a Latin inscription. He'd explained it to her at a barbecue where they had paired under a tree, where others had not approached because it was assumed they were an item. She had listened carefully. His keen, sun-scathed face had demanded her comprehension. Now, doubly offended, she could not salvage what he had so meticulously clarified. She traced the head in the white whizzing vehicle. Minutes later it turned off along the unsealed road to the beach.

Kerri gazed out at the lake alongside her. A fisherman standing in a pirogue suddenly looked helpless. Heavy cloud dusted the surface giving the illusion of rain. Light spitting flecked the windscreen and Jones turned on the wipers precipitately.

'You call that rain, Jones? Turn them off.'

She did turn back. Marco's Suzuki had vanished. Right now he would be churning toward numb villages of idleness and toil, past smiling cripples sent out to beg for coins. In twenty minutes he would pull up to the beach hut of whoever had invited him for a thrown-together lobster lunch. He would sit over the hazy sea after a swim, joining in guiltless and hungry conversation.

Now elephant grass shot up, its pace halted only by gullies flanking the roadway. From time to time a passage led away knitted into it, or battered palm leaves sheltered a table of worn papaya. There was a mad woman who recurred before one of the villages and, sure enough, she was there again today, her fury trapped in filth and idiocy, her womanhood stark and eroded.

Before Winneba there was a series of villages. They wore the stench of the smoked fish they produced, these were curled in piles on tables. Even on Sundays the marketplaces smarted with exchange. Women, roused from sleep on benches, pocketed coins and overlooked stirred children. Barber shop boys lounged on steps. Massive stacks of charcoal lay about like the carcasses of beasts. At the last village Kerri's sudden thirst took the better of her. She pointed out a blue wood-latticed bar with a banner of enticing beer labels.

"We'll stop here, Jones, please.'

Jones, unhappily, brought forth one of Harriet's cast-off Swatches. It was a Hawaiian setting with a bright orange hand jigging around the face.

'But Miss Harriet she say be there before eleven. It is almost eleven now, you see.'

Considerable practice – and love – must have gone into Jones' comprehension of the watch; Kerri could barely decipher it.

'Oh? Harriet just said to get a move on. I want a drink, Jones, not a five-course meal.'

Against her better knowledge Kerri ordered a beer at the bar. Jones overcame his obligations to Harriet and ordered a Malta Guinness, a gruesomely sweet imitation of what the Irish made best. Kerri drank thirstily, her throat parched after the air-conditioned ride and her neck tension already simmering into sweat. Her skin oozed; even Jones' filling pores indicated the leap in temperature.

'You know what we're doing out here, Jones?'

'No – Madame didn't say.'

It remained an indecency to speak about what would shatter neither of their lives. Kerri grasped an image of the common suburban street back home, then visualised a mother, frozen, confronting the tyranny of the phone. If Kerri could undo this event – make it fiction? She slumped back on a stool, the beer had cracked her nerve.

'A guy has drowned at the beach. We have to bring him back to town.'

'Oh, I'm sorry, Madame. I'm very sorry,' said Jones without any particular effort. Kerri, staggered, dared to admire his composure. Were Africans better with dying, because they were so cheated by life?

'I lost my first son in the sea six years ago now. The sea is very dangerous,' Jones said by rote.

Kerri, diminished, offered condolences. Then, prodded by the alcohol, Kerri sampled the parabola of her own expectations and found they were poky, involuted, charmless. She rattled the change in her pocket, ashamed that Leo Farquhar's death would serve as a tangent to another personal shake-down. Perhaps she and Harriet might attain the appropriate state of grief on some boozed-out, motionless night. Perhaps the site of his extinction would set off a pain she could measure at least: in the act of combing it down. She paid. She and Jones walked out from shelter into the fumy sun.

'Kerri! Jones! Kerri Toomey! Calling Kerri Toomey of Abacus Australia! Where the fuck are you?'

Immediately Jones opened Kerri's door, his face in the process of collapse. Kerri took up the receiver. She heard out the spray of expletives.

'I was just checking and I hear you're NOT in your vehicle and you're NOT even at the accident site! This isn't a bloody tourist trek! Don't you realise that poor guy's body's gunna stink to high heaven the longer it stays under the sun? Where the fuck are you now?'

'I took a leak, Harriet. We're on our way. I can see the Winneba tower from here. We'll be there in ten minutes.'

Harriet cut off. Jones, aware of his alliances, refused to make eye contact with Kerri any longer. Kerri breathed deeply, staring at the scalded scrub. Moments later the first buildings of Winneba struggled past. They were poor, shaken survivors of the colonial era, barely dressed in stucco facades, mauled fretwork, buckled verandahs. Some had been remodelled to incorporate small, odd stores. There was a sense of fervent misuse of materials: a doom. A grandiose entranceway was now stacked with vegetable oil cans. Old women bickered on a railless terrace. Revealingly, some of the rooves were caved in, where life continued crudely. A small girl stood to watch them pass.

Jones took the road through the town swiftly. Winneba had known heady days in the seventies when it shared prominence with Dixcove beach as a centre for high-life music. High-life was a type of calypso, brassy beat with its own elaborate dance. Other Africans flocked to the area – Nigerians, Ivorians, Togolese, Beninois, Liberians. It was the pan-African epoch, before the gangrene of megalomania and wacky aid programmes diffused. And what a better site for a brief revival of African brotherhood then this, the cradle of the diaspora? For further west along the coast were the old, insidious slave forts of Cape Coast and Elmina. Kerri had smelt where these bleached white bastions armed with cannons fell to mouldy, lightless dungeons on bedrock. Here the slaves were massed in choked, diseased fear before their voyages to new cruelty.

Jones had arrived at the hotel grounds bordering the beach. He swept under the bright pink gateway toward a spread of mottled bungalows. There were no personnel, no faces visible through the office window, no clients heading to the shore. Kerri's nerves constricted, her very heart shrunken and tight. Only one four-wheel drive stood far off, as close as one could park to the labour of the waves. The tall, headless palms from there commenced their sad parade along the coast. Jones curved the van across.

But why should death in this place still shock her? Thousands, probably hundreds of thousands of lives had dissolved in these waters: the limp, typhus-raged slaves flung into the green wash, and centuries later, fishermen's bloated trunks delivered onto the sand. Kerri stepped outside onto the gravel, her hair tangling in her face. The waves were brilliant. They gathered from the rich deep then thrust over, structureless and fizzling, pretending innocence and noisy play. The sun knifed.

'There is someone that way, Miss,' Jones pointed.

It wasn't that she had not seen them. There were bags. And a crumpled towel laid out. There must have been a figure behind one of the palms. Jones strode off, already making a reckoning about their distance from the van.

'We can go down with this car. Though it might get stuck in the sand. You got chain in the back like Miss Harriet?'

'Of course, Jones,' she said.

They walked down the grassy slope together. As the tufts became harsher, more separate, they found they were walking on fine dry sand between the palms. They progressed. Kerri saw a squatting figure. She saw a body under a beach towel. Tennis shoes and two green coconuts pegged down corners that the wind teased.

A young, pale woman looked up, saying something feebly. Kerri stepped forth to join their rite.

GORGEOUS EYES

A world famous photographer flew in to our hotel to savour the native landscape. She was a harried, shrill-eyed nicotine addict who walked with a careless beat. I took an instant dislike to her charmless appeal. My wife did not.

Initially, the woman photographer appeared at a brisk hour in the morning salon, where she would draw deeply on French cigarettes and serve herself coffee. Food did not appear to interest her at such an hour, although one of the girls – Mercy Obede – later claimed she saw her put bread rolls into deep khaki pockets. I did not see this occur. The first tentative times I saluted her she had cords stringing from her ears and the distracted, if sought-after, expression of one appreciating the higher reaches of classical music. I desisted sharply from attempts at communication. She walked out of the hotel doors with a bold step, ignorant of flashy doormen and prompt drivers, flexing through foliage toward the public taxi rank on the street.

I assume the woman went about her business in the chaotic town. Of Africa's western cities, ours is one of the quieter, more tolerable postings. The days are sudden, breaking in a display of cheap liquid light and rowdy taxis. The plant life is agile, greedy. If left unchecked vines will arrest buildings; in a month a roadway will desiccate. I've often thought that if the people here are thrifty, calamitous, morose, it is because the climate works upon their jaundiced, resistant lives. Perhaps it is the case for all of us.

It is Mercy Obede who procures a copy of the famous photographer's latest art book. A few days into her stay, on a still afternoon, I peruse its contents. The woman is called Nina Cooke. She is a resident of no country, a claimant of no distinctive culture. For thirty years she has prodded the world with her testy Hasselblad (pictured as an emblem after the Introduction hyperbole). She has won prizes, shaken the hands of illiterate chiefs, consumed pigs' trotters, cooked lilies and groggy palm wine with respectful relish. In short, one is obliged to conclude, this woman has constructed an original, feisty life.

I turn the thick coloured pages, perfectly grained. For the uninitiated, the first images show high-shouldered Turkana boys – erotic in beaded body harnesses – mustering cows on an unyielding landscape. Eye glances are caught, modelled, injected with the photographer's obvious flair. And yet for the seasoned watcher, for one who knows how these boys play soccer, wish for jobs, are balmy with discontent, the dying exotica becomes a crucible of sadness. I glance on, frowning. If Nina Cooke's gift ever needed an honest name it would be the invasive trivialisation of humble detail. It appears she is at the vanguard of a vulgar world trait.

My wife Margaret enters my office as I close the photographer's book. She wears the electric, upheaved expression that fuels the engine of my love for her. Her eyes fall on the book's final image – a Muslim desert woman whose private loss becomes jaded haute couture.

'Oh Darling! Have you met her already? Don't you think she's marvellous? I don't believe we've ever had anyone as culturally rich as her. She's devastating – such a force. She says she wants to photograph my eyes.'

'What?'

I am not an envious man by design, but the exploration of Margaret's eyes I feel is my exclusive right.

'My eyes, Olivier. Nina says I have gorgeous eyes. She wants to photograph them.'

I light a cigarette, considering Margaret. There are times when her naïvety astounds me. A woman of fifty regresses terribly, she will fold into her girlhood with a possessed innocence. Several times, since her operation, Margaret has become infatuated with sultry men who ignore her.

'You'll have to charge her a fee,' I say, turning the thing on its head to quell my sudden, unreasonable anger.

'Whatever for? Are you joking? This woman is an artist. This is a privilege Olivier. Don't assume you have to manage my interests.'

Margaret has become haughty, distressed. I turn the book around to her. In her grasp it falls open on the page of a young Somali bride, modestly dressed, surrounded by pugnacious sisters.

'Do you see?' I attempt. 'This book is a glossy celebration of Africa's cruelty. That woman is about to be raped by her fifty year old groom. She has been circumcised by those women surrounding her. She will know pain for the rest of her life.'

My wife looks at me with true horror. She shuts the book.

'Olivier, you have never understood beauty.'

Some time later Mercy Obede passes through the door. I see the intensity of my brooding mirrored in her unclear eyes. She places a blank envelope on the desk and enquires whether I should like coffee or tea. Disturbed, I am unwilling to answer her; I dismiss her with a gesture I suspect I will later regret. Directly outside my window a new gardener is severing a tall plant presently guarding my shoulder from the later sunlight. I unfasten the window to check the youth, but find the sliced, now bleeding protuberance a dozen centimetres short of my face.

On my rounds of the hotel I find the usual spartan fervour

under way. Kofi in the souvenir shop salutes me, handing me a fresh copy of *Le Monde*. In my hands it is still tinged with an aircraft's plush, metallic scent. Scanning the troubled headlines, I sense the world's dreary nonchalance, its garbled nitpicking. At the reception desk three superb Ivorians man telephones and direct shabby tourists to the coconut grove bar. Their myriads of synthetic plaits turn under fluorescent light; their painted fingernails skit out from black, seamed hands. At their backs, on masonite stylised with a design that I loathe, five clocks announce the time in significant world cities, reminding the keener of us the extent of our blessed state.

For an instant I turn on my heel. I have seen Margaret heading toward the pool area holding a large hat and magazine. I presume she has played sport, or chatted with women friends in the interlude following our meeting. She walks along the pebblecrete in a pair of flattering Italian clogs, wearing a Tuereg anklet I have not seen before.

I am feeling wistful toward her: harsh and yet reluctant to give new fuel to my harshness. When we deeply disagree, the tissue of our union grows stains that do not dispel when our physical grace resumes. Margaret enters a phase of terse frigidity. I sense the shameful urge to conquer. Blindly, I turn through the foyer toward the bar, where I accept a glass of iced water from one of the waiters.

To my left a familiar khaki-clad figure emits smoke and clutches a drink. It is the international photographer, in person, no doubt reviving after an assault on the town's graphic resources. I deliberate my utter unwillingness to speak with her, until delayed good sense allows me to perceive what is actually occurring. Some previous conversation has taken place between herself and the young waiter. Angrily, I see how her continued stare renders the man's back tight and conscious. I send the man on a futile mission to the kitchens.

Unperturbed, the woman delves into a horrid, practical-looking tote bag. She retrieves a sachet of lens-cleaning tissues. Having perused her book less than an hour ago, I have the feverish sensation that she has taken our intimacy for granted, so that even our silence assumes a perverted quality. I am appalled. It is Mercy Obede's grave appearance that alters our poses. I am summoned to the exchange bureau.

In the evening Margaret's attendance at an ambassadorial cocktail is not essential, but merely an act of good form. I approach her in the generous suite that is our home.

'Why Margaret – have you forgotten the Spanish cocktail this evening? I believe Ernest is already in the lobby.'

Margaret looks at me over a spicy ginger drink she prepares for her throat.

'I thought I'd sit it out tonight, Olivier. I haven't the strength. You know how my back gives out at those functions. I don't think I could bear to hear another frightful national day speech.'

As proof she extends herself along the settee, allowing me to study the tremouring anklet I'd noticed before. I comment upon it.

'Why Olivier – it's from Nina. The woman you misunderstand. You don't like it on me?'

Given the context, the anklet appears the cheapest, gaudiest trinket. But I will not be a weasel for easy bait.

'What a pity. I'm afraid I will have to leave you, Margaret.'

Throughout the cocktail party I feel a migraine headache developing behind my left eye socket. I am a tall man, and make a conscious effort to defer the current of pain from my tensed facial muscles. As a consequence the pain devours my concentration, and begins to needle the fibres of my neck. I feel as though I am pitted in a stance of defence before the Spanish Ambassador, a sober forty-five year old at odds with my ill-managed replies. To a degree, she too has been entranced by the international photographer.

'I hear you've changed the flavour of the month down your way. Quite an honour to have such an art house figure in the vicinity,' she very nearly contemplates.

'Yes – although hers is the most deadening form of art.'

'I beg pardon?'

Here I oscillate, unwilling to pan out my view for another bout of strife.

'The quality is unforgiving. Her eye is remorselessly – *able.*'

The comment nettles her. We accept further drinks The Spanish woman recounts of having met Nina in a previous posting, and then pauses over details she suspects I am loath to hear. A frank, lesser diplomat from the Middle East arrives to offer his greetings. My host's attention necessarily diverts.

As soon as the first guests exit from beneath the sweltering canopy I salute the ring of fellow expatriates and work my way into the moist yard. A jewelled Indian woman passes me, and for no reason gives me a humoured, exquisite smile. Bothered by the heady charm of her culture I examine my own innocence. Had I approached her with stealth, with mystery? A repulsed incomprehension overwhelms me. I hurry toward the car while another foreign anthem tolls through the palms.

Although I had hoped for Margaret's absence from our apartment I feel piqued by it upon arrival. I take two of the stronger cachets from a packet we share – both lifelong migraine sufferers. My face in the mirror lacks the degree of credibility one persistently imagines one is wearing. In such brittle moments, my claim upon Margaret is intense. As soon as the pain thaws, I resolve to bewitch her once again.

It is just on nine o'clock. The restaurant salon is in full swing. Businessmen on shaky contracts hunch over gravy. Nigerians sever steaks. Mixed youthful groups fluctuate between menu choices. My innate fear is that Margaret is in a quiet, enclosed space away from all of this. She is perhaps in the other woman's room, her shadow cast on the hessian wallpaper, her coy eyes in fruitful exchange. I recall Nina Cooke's room number, two floors below our own. Then bravely check my thoughts: if treachery were always so harmless!

The staff sense I am agitated. Mercy Obede, chief unpicker of my moods, glances at me from her post at the restaurant entrance. She wears a falsely obtuse expression, keeping the boys from me warily. What I might thank her for turns to sharp, groundless reprimand when a glass slides from a tray, scattering noisily. Mercy ushers the cleaner across, admonishes the sore waiter, avoids the clamour of my stare.

I pass outdoors to the pool area. Immediately the air, pungent and humid, settles its weight upon my shoulders. I stride across the pebblecrete to the far, bare end of the pool. A light, not unlike a tranquil, venomous medusa, sends rays through the water. Mosquitoes whine in the tossed palms behind me. Under a canopy diners fold and unfold menus, whilst fans whirr the thick air in unison. Inevitably, my eyes are pulled upward over the building's uncomplicated tiled facade. Like all successful architecture on this continent it fails to overreach. The emblem of the hotel chain is outlined in blue neon on the roof, with the hotel's name in blunt, familiar characters. These elements undoubtably daunt the city's poor skyline.

As I presumed, the curtains are drawn across the window of Nina Cooke's room on the fifth floor. The bedside lamps are switched on, daubing the hessian curtains with light. I am certain my wife is therewithin, her green-spiced eyes lured open, photographed, explained. My panic is compounded by the sudden return of pain in my forehead. For no reason I remember the practice of blood-letting, and wonder if men inflamed with ardour felt relief when hot trickles crept across their flesh. Then, in a swift change of thought provoked by the snap of cutlery, I begin combating my more temporal thoughts. Had Nina Cooke ever married? Had she ever tasted that harmful, exacerbated state whilst fumbling with the world? Had she carried a child as my wife had, and seen it expelled into gloved hands, ugly with vernix? Or had her own bandwagon of images sufficed her?

One of the waiters, a soft, secure man named Ben, approaches me. He asks should I like a light meal, or one of my preferred drinks. Earlier on in the year Ben's attractive daughter fell pregnant to a French researcher staying here, who toyed with the idea of an exotic marriage. As much as I respect Ben's services and predictable character, I advised the young man to leave money with the girl, camouflage his intentions, and pursue his lifeplan where he belongs. Although my mixed marriage might claim otherwise, I am no herald of cultural watering-down, nor suffering hybrids. The French researcher vanished; Ben's daughter will eventually marry a scoundrel of her own kind. Ben looks at me, engrossed with the possible severity of my silence.

'No thanks, Ben. I'll take a nightcap in my room. Good evening.'

'Yes please, Sir.'

I return to the lobby. I take the empty elevator up to Nina Cooke's floor. I walk out onto the carpet and take the hall the length of the building. Several meal trays sit in front of doors – skewiff plates and half-glasses of beer. I sense that the need for food has been replaced by desire, masturbation, cable TV. Before Nina Cooke's door I pause, in great pain, my skin tacky with sweat. There is a silence I am incapable of gauging. Perhaps, at intervals, I hear the slight click of a camera shutter. But I have no certainty of this. I imagine I hear bedclothes shuffle, one or two murmurs. And yet – thank God! – my imagination remains sightless.

But then I do hear Margaret stammer, in the lacking voice she uses when shy:

'Is that all right. Shall I take it up again?'

Nina replies, her voice fervent, coaching.

'Again? Of course – I want – Yes, like that. You are divine like that. Do you believe in former lives? I feel certain you were a primped-up marquise with a satin-rounded bust – I'm sure I've seen those drenched eyes elsewhere. In Velasquez? Yes, but don't snicker, I want boldness, roundness; big pupils. Think of the last time you had an orgasm! That's it. More now. Imagine you have a set of young hot lips down there, setting it alight. I want to see that heat. Let me see fire...'

I fall into the ensuing silence as a body into rubble.

Some time later there is a burst of fractured female laughter, alcohol or lust-induced, beyond the door. I recognise Margaret's joy, released at such an exorbitant cost. I feel the sensation of being hunted by my own master.

Quickly, I pace down the empty hallway to the lift. The silver doors open, revealing my destroyed face on the reflective panel inside. To my left I see Mercy Obede, hands grasped together, her face turned from the nudity of my emotion. I am alarmed and irritated by her presence. As the doors cushion together she reminds me of the arrival of an eminent Nigerian writer, just off the plane from Zurich. I swear in my own tongue, sensing Margaret's estrangement as something now orchestrated – and nearly public. Mercy bows guardedly. We resume poses of perfect detachment before the lift discharges us into the lobby.

I find the Nigerian writer altogether too brash. Patiently, I listen to the rundown of European illuminaries so reluctant to see him depart. The man amuses himself with a few anecdotes I fail to appreciate, and rather bossily suggests we have a drink. I am at the point of refusing when I see Margaret and Nina idling toward Margaret's driver Ernest, now in semi-slumber by the front desk. I believe I make out the name of a nightclub – trashy, but not the trashiest – and a message to be passed on to myself, Monsieur Olivier. The ladies depart. I find myself in a perplexed lull, obedient to the Nigerian. He sends his bags upstairs and leads me to a table in the bar. The pianist nearby ripples melancholy notes above the fracas, such that one unthinkingly recalls regret.

'A fine crowd for a weeknight,' my guest muses. 'And your pianist – quite a style.'

The peculiar elements of this evening have worn down my tendency to isolate myself, so that the writer's tentative comments strike a lax note. Drink, or the music, has subdued his post-airport harrying. He sinks into the vinyl seat, now amiable.

'This hotel hasn't changed in two decades. Most of our white elephants from the seventies are now in shambles,' he rightly says.

'We do our best to counter the elements,' I offer.

Tasting my scotch, my own impulse is to plumb the reaches of my love for Margaret. In its condensed form it resembles obsession; viewed from afar it appears as tired, tainted attraction. I measure our present sex against our vehemence of the past. As with the intricacy of shells, our love now hides a gritty nexus; many empty chambers.

The writer frowns at my obvious distraction.

'It appears you have an illustrious guest in your books. Nina Cooke on her rounds again.'

'Yes,' I respond barely.

'Still going, that woman. She does sell well in Europe,' he speaks with a writer's nastiness. I am alerted.

'When my second book came out she tried it on me – the

absorbing portrait business. When I saw the photos I was horrified at the way she'd put her label on me – the way she'd interpreted me according to the flavour of the day. Many have said the same of her. I've heard that when she travels in the bush she gives trinkets to the kids and photographs of herself to the chiefs –'

'Colonialisation of the press? Held as art?' I suggest.

The writer laughs. One of his historical books, I recall, stages a modern African revolution, complete with the hideous slaughter of whites.

'Correct,' he grins. 'For this is the new age of spiritual execution. You have hit on it.'

He stands, walks over to the pianist and speaks to him. The music changes to a jazzed-up Chopin.

'Can't help myself,' he explains. 'That old cultural imperialism knows no bounds.'

We pass a couple of hours together before the pianist retires and the building's silence ushers us to bed. We shake hands in the elevator at his floor. I watch him advance down the hallway, key poised in hand. Throughout our conversation I have not been in a position to view Margaret's re-entry. Mercifully, my headache has eased, though traces of it simmer as I anticipate sighting her, smelling her; seizing her.

I find the apartment permeated with Margaret's scent. She is scrolled up on the bedside; she coughs lightly. Trousers, her loose cotton shirt and overshirt, a black brassiere, have all been thrown on an upholstered chair. Her jewellery is laid out on the dresser – silver Tuereg earrings with twin garnets, an embroidered pendant, a heavy ring. I pass into the bathroom. Various used cotton wool balls show she has removed make-up. The jars are unsettled; surfaces wear prints. Undressing quietly, I reflect upon how we have terminated the evening: myself in the company of the teasing writer; Margaret latched to Nina Cooke's arm in the smoke of a lurid bar. Our remoteness appears the more obtuse.

I lower myself into the bed next to the orb of her back. What if this were the last night we were to spend together? What if this were our last chance to embrace, to fretfully embrace? I inhale my slumbering wife's odour. The idea of sleep suddenly feels akin to that of loss, even death's sullen fall. If I should ever lose her? I begin to tremble. Then, daringly, I clasp her, aware of a sudden clench.

'Olivier! At this hour! Do leave off –'

My wife merely turns, removing herself from me. I am left at the border of the landscape of sleep.

The following morning Margaret is tricky. Her attitude is hard to accept, given my heavy, exhausted mood. She is, in a way, help-ful, But her handing me coffee is part of a play, a new deal. Her naked hands fidget.

'Olivier – what on earth were you up to last night? Who was the extravagant guest that kept you out until all hours?'

'I should think you enjoyed a more extravagant evening over-all.'

In my weariness my feelings for Margaret approach dislike. She wears a shapeless beige shirt, a pendant of manacled glass beads. I feel certain she is braless and this idea now fills me with distaste.

'You know Olivier, I don't know why you have this caged bear attitude toward Nina. She's just a highflyer, she appreciates the right to exist. I've never been so surprised by your backwardness. In any case you shan't be able to redeem yourself. Nina's decided to head off on tonight's flight. She's off up north to tackle the Bedouins in the Spanish Sahara. Of course it will be murderously hot –'

'And that's a cause for this inane cheerfulness?'

'Olivier –' she braces. 'You did read my letter? I gave it to Mercy yesterday afternoon. I am surprised it didn't reach you. I warn you I'll not be writing another.'

She rises, her sails a little less rotund than before, a quaver in her bottom lip. I straighten the day-old newspaper whilst she pauses.

'I have an appointment with Nina for breakfast,' she concludes patchily, and exits.

Immediately I recall the plain envelope delivered to my office yesterday afternoon. My memory is perpetually sharp, though I am astonished I neglected to open it. I page Mercy Obede to have it brought to my room at once. In no mood for Margaret's play-act-ing, I do however, fall victim to a sudden spell of fear, such that accompanies a summons by authority. I feel quite weak by the time a careful Mercy Obede knocks at the door and hands over the unmarked envelope. Crashing the door closed, I lurch toward the breakfast table, my thick black fingers unfolding the single page.

Dear Olivier, commences my beloved wife's hand,

Do not presume to resist –

THE SEVERED REEF

May 16 1989 NAIROBI: Australian Embassy officials have released the name of a man critically wounded in a bomb attack on a sugar mill near Kisimaayo, in southern Somalia. Paul Maddox, 34, of Narrabeen, Sydney, worked on an internationally sponsored project to develop the country's agricultural resources. The blast claimed the life of a Somali co-worker.

Until these last few moments Paul had believed himself a type of seafarer. That he would find himself violently seasick on a fishing boat in the Indian Ocean, off another crust of the world, had not appeared in his scheme of things. Dazed, he looked around for Abdi at the stern. Abdi was sitting abreast the noisy engine, now sharing a cigarette with the impish fisherman.

It wasn't the first time Paul had seen them engage in this type of social snakes and ladders. Often, they would drop down a few notches as Abdi had done now or, in the inverse, limber up to merge with the terse, self-conscious elite. Paul had seen housegirls interrupt ministerial meetings, and humble drivers embraced by men of great stature. He had no way of interpreting these brief charades. He continued to watch Abdi pally with the fisherman who an hour earlier, had appeared to him as imbecile and tubercular. They chatted like an unevenly built couple of brothers, the man's hands occasionally drawing on the wheel, a complicity uniting them.

Paul retched once again, feeling the weave of his hardened muscles. In an hour none of them had so much as cast out a line. It was the tuna season. Occasionally, bursts of shadow carved the swells, scoring the surface with a spray of fins. As the boat rose and dropped, puttering nonsensically, it seemed as fruitlessly involved in a similar exertion.

His eyes went out to the vigorous sea, the way it tugged and ployed the vessel. It was the cut blue of a stone, involved in a fiery refraction with the high sun. He knew the scalps of the Africans were shielded by coiling hair the thickness of wool. Paul's thinning crown, no doubt reddening now, elucidated, attracted its rays as overtly as a bloody car bonnet. Hot enough to scorch eggs. Once more he doused himself, looking to the eroded land. On other coastlines, resorts, mansions and restaurants had annihilated ecosystems. Here a shawled woman trailed a camel along, amphore on her shoulders. Even from the boat, rocking, Paul knew that if she spotted his white skin the woman would try to sell him her smoked milk or her amber beads, for a fistful of their doctored currency.

Abdi, his discourse with the fisherman at an end, came up to where Paul was crouched, shading his eyes with an old air ticket. Abdi bent next to him. The odour of sweat and spiciness came up close. Abdi flicked his cigarette into the churns and released the frankest part of him – his blanched palms – into gestures.

'I see you're not up to it today. A pity you see, our fisherman says that yesterday they had an exceptional haul. Though the sea's bounty, and our luck, are no ingredients for certain success. Can you see the river delta opening up there? A sight yes, but surely Australia's coasts offer similar delights. No doubt more... cured? Can one say that? Several of us were of the idea that tourism could be developed along these stretches. A shuttle service from the airport at Kis'mayo, to be enlarged of course. Small groups you see. The type of thing they started off with at Malindi in Kenya. More doggedly than most will admit, considering malaria persists as strongly there as here. What should you say, Paul, to outlay costs of fifteen or twenty million? Hut style, I am visualising. Pity the only Italians with their fingers on pulse points are bent on trolleying lobsters to restaurants in Milan... Ridiculous hopes, I guess you understood well before I learned...'

Abdi hoisted his buttocks onto the only crossbeam the boat provided, jointing the gunwales close to the bow. His listener edged into this crux alternately bracing and arching away from him, as the boat pulleyed on the waves.

Presently, Abdi called to the fisherman in their guttural voice, a voice that burred deep in their throats. In English, he turned to Paul:

'The reefs here, are very shallow and irregular. I thought I saw an outcrop. You have heard, no doubt, the story of the Russian port project, abandoned fifteen unhappy years ago at least? Their thoughtful dumping of concrete blocks all but destroyed the coral reefs outside the capital, and guaranteed no further protection for the rest of the coast. The Indian Ocean, of course, is known for her secret maladies. Much more evilly thought of than your Pacific, I have perceived, though I believe you have a similar problem with sharks off the Sydney coast... Is that not right? And are not the Australians regarded as experts in the field? I recall a team of men in sunhats – the type you should be wearing now – who came and set off explosives in the waters outside the capital. An enterprise, for all who came to see the hacked fish blown to high heaven. Then I believe they packed up and went home... Mission accomplished, isn't that what is said?'

Paul sensed Abdi's eyes somewhere on his shirt, his scalp, and then openly, on his face. It was perhaps the first time in months their eyes had locked. Today Paul's green eyes squinted, one lid enlarged with a stye. Paul knew he was weakened, putrid, disarmed. If this were the culmination – here in the bloody sea, in this vile puttering boat – Paul might have found the strength to be glad of it. At least that would be it and he could be released from this. But Abdi's dark eyes, their rims merging to blue, merging to milk, were too sober this time for Paul to feel anything other than the incompleteness of their drama. Abdi's stare withered, and Paul looked down to his splattered jeans.

The water sprayed them both. Close they were, to a rush of breakers indicating the reef. It was as near as the excursion would go to the threatening swells. Abdi motioned a hand behind him, barely guiding its movement, as he watched a riff of seagulls disinterestedly.

They had been more convivial once. At the outset of Paul's term, two years ago, Abdi had hardly disguised excitement at the fact that his counterpart on the grapefruit project would not be a European, but a man from a colonised country as himself. It made for some healthy debates in those first days when Paul – before Claudia flew out – stayed at the Makka Hotel. Abdi had a flashy, slouchy way of entering the sham foyer, saluting the headwaiter, who would see them to a table among the palms. Paul enjoyed the off-guarded banter, the drink, the bashful, smirking girls. Hearing Abdi's high snigger for the first time brought on the sensation that Paul was flirting with a new lover, and ahead lay all the delicious moments of an affair. Africans of his earlier acquaintance were almost as a rule short, pungent, excessively polite men who set about engaging his attention. And yet the first few times Abdi let Paul peruse his features Paul felt a type of arousal, and knew that this man would come to tap his most immediate impulses. At first he wondered if it weren't sexual, when Abdi's palm like a naked object made flint of his forearm. But Abdi had a way of releasing him when the moment was through, and Paul learnt that that was all of it.

Immediately, Paul felt a need to know this man. One afternoon when he'd moved into the house, he asked Abdi to bring around his wife, Khadija, and young daughter, Saifa. Paul felt buoyant. He had the maid prepare grapefruit juice and open some bottles of Coke. He worried whether Abdi would drink beer in front of his wife. Or if the little one would settle for the last of his imported biscuits. When they entered, Abdi first, the woman shyly, the child bauble-eyed – Paul's own woodenness settled on his guests. It was an abrupt afternoon. Paul grew irritated at the wife's belittled attitude and refusal to talk. I couldn't have been Abdi's fault. Abdi nursed his hands as if conscious of the old abyss pushing them apart. It would never work then, in this way, but at least Abdi gave him a look that said there were other avenues to try.

From the beginning their adjacent offices were located on the Ministry of Agriculture's seventh floor. In each office the blocky, rusted furniture was arranged identically. They were gifts of old Eastern bloc allies. Initially, Paul was baffled as to why both desks were veered away from the impressive and, he would have thought, inspiring view. Surf pounded the old port walls spectacularly. As he might have guessed, the window was jammed, the air conditioner faulty, and thus the high room reached terrific temperatures. His secretary was hardly capable of typing English on the bulky Russian relic someone had thoughtfully bolted to the desk.

The Somalis had a gesture, a beautiful one. At ten usually, for the workday commenced early, the men left their secretaries and descended to the street. Theirs was a central building, close to a gathering ground where men of all ages and variations of dress stood, squatted, leant on gnarled sticks, gesticulated and discussed, all the while sipping glasses of shai or gingery coffee bought from boys skitting between them. Until midday prayers, this was the most vigorous tract of the city centre. Abdi would lead Paul away from here as though mischief were involved. But they only went on to the crumbly Arab quarter. Abdi, in front, negotiated alleyways and rocky squares, while bothered women scrubbing garments observed them. Occasionally, Paul peered through doorways to the dugout rooms: utensils might be crocked upon a bench, or a sleeping body bent up on the earth. More often, Paul watched Abdi's tight polyester trousers, and the way his heels became chalkier and whiter as he advanced. Then there would be the gesture, usually at the door of the bar they frequented. Abdi would turn around, the raw strong sky including and blackening him: the hand would upturn gently as if to say Well? So what is it to be? And Paul would join him.

Inside the bar was painted blue, with only a few stools and tables. Paul was aware it had been a test at first. Abdi ordered two oily Scotch eggs which the boy dunked out with a hand. The Australian resisted the impulse to throw up. In time, the men were able to joke about Paul's expression as he lifted the meat-encrusted egg to his mouth, and further on, in hindsight, Paul was even grateful for these moments.

*

What Paul had in mind when he invited Abdi to dinner – alone – was twofold: he wanted to include the man in the only social set-up he knew; he also wanted to show the man off. And yet, in the light of what would happen, Paul's view of Abdi would commence its pivot.

At the table that night were Monique, a French divorcee; Barton and his wife from the dam project; Andreas, a tall Dutch fellow recently arrived; and Shamsa and Osman, a couple of Somali doctors of his lengthy acquaintance. Abdi joined in the discussion ably, no stranger to expatriate palaver. Paul saw him as wry, stimulated, not yet embittered. Would he be able to shirk his future? Before the wine set in Paul glanced around for Abdi's reaction to the lobster soup, the grilled snapper, the showy fruit meringue dessert. Abdi, the dark miraculous skin of his eyelids gently lowered, leant his forearm on the back of Monique's chair. It was the most suggestive gesture of the evening. Not, Paul thought, because he himself desired the woman. No – what excited Paul was the way he saw the woman's knuckled creamy back differently, all of a sudden. Paul was infused with a desire, which he took to be Abdi's desire refracted through him. Did Abdi want Monique? Could he have, he would have offered her to his friend. For Paul's eyes were quickly full of the Somali riding her on his bed.

Hours later, on the hammocks outside, mosquitoes crossing the humid air between them, Paul was thrown back when Abdi revealed his complete innocence of women.

'So how is it that your wife... your Claudia?... does not have a baby every time? Do you use those rubber fingers that they sell here?'

He spoke fumblingly, milking dry his glass of scotch, no aversion, no reluctance to opening this new topic between them.

'My wife she complains you know. Oh she complains long and hard! She always scared, always tight you know. She stitched like a sandal my Khadija. She dry as the Juba in March...'

Paul was shocked, repulsed. He knew the women here and in Sudan, and some persistent parts of Muslim Africa, were crudely, cruelly circumcised. Habitually, he shrank from whites whom he considered, had a voyeuristic interest in the violation. Women who talked of it, seethingly, reactionary groups who showed short, obscene documentaries. Paul thought of it as a private pain, somehow overcome as only tradition knew how. He had never conjured it in terms of sexual rapport, or birth, or menstruation. Or Abdi and Khadija. Paul's shock would hover behind their future exchanges.

A few weeks after the dinner Claudia was booked out on a

flight from Rome. It stalled Paul's thinking, knowing she would enter his life once more. For Claudia hated their life together in Africa. She grew thin here; her health was touchy. Matters had not been helped by Paul's infidelity in another country, and the embarrassing way the couple's exploits had come to light. Claudia had taken the affair like a sinker to her soul, and Paul feared the debt to her would crumble the life in him.

For Claudia's sake he paid for membership at the English and American clubs at the beach. Almost exclusively white-patronised, both provided refuge from the havoc outside. Deckchairs and drinks, a bitumen tennis court; slouchy ball boys. People spent a lot of energy harping about the country's ills. Some, having experienced more comfortable postings, complained about the heat, the erratic power and water supplies, the complete absence of anything even the humblest Westerner could crave. Amusement rippled around their send-ups of broad, dopey housegirls. Happy hours, disco nights, rounds of cards and chess were arranged. Prostitutes circled the entrance door at the end of the week. Paul began to spend more time than he might have wished at the bar, or in a group of chairs close to the pool, fixed in the jovial type of silence. It would only be until Claudia found her feet again, he told himself.

Quite suddenly, Paul found himself in a morass with Abdi. It was when the President dug in his heels, daring Westerners to abandon the country. A cruel play was evolving: as inflation rocketed, the price of sugar or flour or rice could leap in a matter of hours. Purchases were made from plastic bags stuffed with bills. Soldiers appeared; stones were thrown in the streets. At night, gunshots tested the quiet.

Of course, Paul and Abdi's collaboration suffered. They began to skip the practice of heading off to the Arab quarter, until it was more usual for each to remain in his office sipping tea fetched by the secretary, with Paul devouring bananas whenever his hunger came on strong. Each time the door handle flipped down and Abdi's tight, colourless shirt advanced into the office, Paul was unable to compose his muscles adequately.

'It is not that we are ungrateful for gifts of rice and oil and sugar that go straight into the Pakistanis' hands, destroying any semblance of the desired market forces. No – no, our markets have long survived on the cheapest, most disrespectful forms of barter. Rather this obsession with loan repayments and our galloping currency, this ridiculous race to the elusive cure – balance, perfection, democracy – what you will... Why pretend this and allow the old devil his global banquet of arms?... Conscripts, our mighty leader now resorts to in his tribal pot-shotting. My brother, it was reported to me today, not an educated man, was dragged by soldiers into a cattle truck around seven this morning. His wife, naturally, is quite convinced already that her children are as good as fatherless...'

Paul had no provisions for this type of discourse. Holding a pencil, he suspected that his was the face of white unscrupulousness.

In May the trip south to oversee the Kisimaayo sugar mill was thrown up. A supervisor down there had died of a heart attack. In view of the stagnation of their own project Paul and Abdi were nominated by the Ministry to make a quick appraisal, as there were some doubts regarding the safety of the area. Paul was eager to depart. It would free him from Claudia, whose thin body unreasonably made him flinch; it would link him to Abdi, whose sore, baffling company he still craved.

He and Abdi set out with a driver for the four hundred kilometre trip south. The road was severely pot-holed and for stretches, truncated from the next uncertain lengths of asphalt. Outside Meerka, the first coastal town, the road gave way to an impassable chasm, work of the dunes edging coastward, pushing the poor topsoil of the adjacent hills before them in a fissured, red fringe. The driver veered through sand gullies and clefts to the beach, and there the low tide allowed them to go ahead with some speed to the old port town.

Abdi might have spent the night here or more justifiably, further on in Brava. These were places that retained much more of their Arab flavour than the hotch-potched capital. Instead they continued along the hostile road parting the landscape. At some point, although no sign indicated the event, the equator was passed. The sun descended quickly and the vehicle halted for the two Muslims to pray. Abdi, a drinker whose religion seldom surfaced, washed his extremities with water the driver offered from a plastic flask. They shared the prayer mat, inclining together, murmuring. When they kissed the earth their pale coupled heels were the only objects of vulnerability before the faint, extinguished horizon.

'So this is the first time you have explored our unfortunate country?'

It was Abdi, turning around in the front seat, now considering him.

'You say you know the sea well. Boats and manoeuvres. Tides and the like. I like most citysiders in Africa have lost whatever hand my ancestors had in such things, though I know for a fact that they were warriors, hardly fishermen. Despite the promise such an industry might hold, were it cultivated by someone less crafty than the Chinese, fishermen are located within our lowest, most servile ranks. Lobsters in fact, that fantasy food of most white palates, are regarded as – let me think – the cockroaches of the sea... Our driver here (did I mention this to you?), is a business man of a sort, and suggests that we contract his brother, a fisher-man, to take us out in his vessel tomorrow morning. He says that most white men passing through here feel a great passion for this sport. Being the tuna season at present, we would be foolish not to initiate you eh?... One thinks of Hemingway, and the last white hunters of Africa and – ha! – realises his paltry prey is now avail-able in cans...'

Paul listened, seizing the skeletal door frame of the govern-ment vehicle. He could only be silent. If it ever came to it, Paul still believed he would have noosed himself to Abdi's fate. That last evening, Paul held onto this.

Now, in the vessel, perhaps the tension had abated. Or at least Abdi's last comments were cuffed by the wind. The Australian tried to breathe deeply, raising his head from where it had been crooked over the bow. He had finished retching, he hoped; his torso began to loosen.

Paul recognised their Land Rover on a prominent dune, and the old sabre-armed watchman they had paid pacing around it, sentry-style. He was the only visible figure on the hot verge of sand above them, and indeed under the luminous sky. The boat surged towards this over the abrupt, clear waves, all occupants in silence.

JOHN GOWER

A JOURNEY
and other stories

JOHN GOWER

Martin Reid

John Gower was born in London in 1953. He works intermittently for the NHS. He has published poems and fiction in various magazines, and over the last eight years his stories have appeared in *Abraxas, Ambit, Inkshed, The North, Panurge, Prospice, Quartz, Stand, Staple,* and *The Wide Skirt,* with others due in *Gairfish* and *Passion.*

WALTZ

The rain is whispering and pattering on the slates above her head.
She's up in the loft, crouched down, picking through the bags and
boxes stuffed with her old belongings. Why has she suddenly
started thinking of him again after all this time? All afternoon she
has felt... There seems no reason for it. She leans forward and
peers at herself in the dusty mirror, puts her fingers to her plump-
ish, forty-year-old face. It's as if something had been dug to the
surface, emotions she has not felt for years slowly taking hold of
her again. She thought all that was long buried, finished with.
Who would have imagined that anything could still be there, after
all this time? That she would feel like this. She undoes another
box, pulls out one or two items, looking at them, putting them
back – a shoe, a hairbrush, a blue leather handbag ... It's strange
to have the past in one's fingers suddenly, to discover that things
which were once a part of oneself have grown old and tired like so
much jumble. She should have got rid of it years ago. She lifts out
a dark crimson dress. A diary drops at her feet. She'd forgotten.
She picks it up. It smells of that damp bedsit in Holland Park. She
opens it, looks at the first entry or two. They mean nothing to her,
speaking of people and events she has long forgotten; even her
handwriting looks unfamiliar, looped and fussy, not like hers at all.
But now she is paging carefully through. She finds what she is
looking for: that week in autumn when they met. Almost guiltily, as
if it is someone else's diary, she begins to read.

For an hour she sits, the diary perched on her knees, the
pages seeming thick and stiff in her fingers. She reads every word
she wrote about him, until each painful memory is in place.
When the entries abruptly cease, leaving the rest of the little book
blank, she finds it hard to believe that the whole thing lasted only
those few months. The way it ended seems as unreal now as it did
then. She remembers going to visit him in the hospital. It was the
last time she saw him. He phoned her and told her it would be
easier for them both. Six weeks later he was dead. She wrote a
foolish letter to his wife which she should never have sent.

She puts the diary back, and holds the dress on her lap, absently
stroking it with her fingers. She thinks of him, of those evenings at
the Empire, of walking back with him through the frosty nights...
It's as if it all happened yesterday.

She looks at her watch, trying to remember what time her hus-
band said he'd be home. The rain is beating down above. The
small loft is filled with the noise. She's cold. She feels tearful and
depressed. She wants to go down, but she can't seem to move. Ever

since she came up she has had the sensation that she is not alone in the house, that someone is down there.

It is late. The wind whips the rain into his face as he crosses the street. The house is in darkness, not a window lit. You'd have thought she'd at least –

He stops.

A figure is slumped on the little front lawn.

He pushes through the gate, hurries over. It is his wife. She is sprawled face down. He crouches beside her. She seems barely conscious.

Struggling to get her up the path to the porch he feels that he is being watched. He glances back into the street. But there is only the rain glittering grey under the lamps. He props her against him, her bare arms dangling as he fumbles for his keys. The trees sigh and tussle in the dark.

Inside he lays her on the sofa and pulls off her shoes. The long crimson dress she is wearing clings to her legs; she's soaked through. He tries again to rouse her, shaking her, but she doesn't stir. Realising he must get her out of the wet dress he rolls her over and begins to undo the buttons down the back. It's of a dark velveteen. It's too small for her. It is not a dress he remembers having seen before; no more than the pearls... Suddenly she turns and drapes a clammy arm around his neck, pulling him close. She mumbles a name. He takes her pallid face between his hands. Her eyes are open now, staring up at him as though woken from a dream. She is sitting up, shivering. He helps her upstairs to the bathroom, runs a hot bath. She stands staring expressionlessly at the flurting taps as he tugs the dress down over her hips. It is as if he isn't there, does not exist.

'All right?' he says.

She has come down in her dressing-gown. She looks drained.

He lights the gas-fire. She sits, watching the white clays begin to glow. The wind blunders in the chimney's throat.

'Where have you *been* for Christ's sake?' he says at last.

Twisting her head, she touches the dark dress draped on the chair beside her, and then picks up the pearls with a vague frown, putting them to her lips.

'*Jill,*' he says.

The rain taps, taps from the guttering outside. She is fingering the dress, examining the little buttons. He snatches it away.

76

Still she does not speak.

A gust of rain clatters on the window. He goes across to close the curtains, and pauses a moment, as though catching sight of something on the front lawn below. The raindrops crawl like jewelry down the pane.

When he turns, the room is empty.

She is halfway up the stairs, her hand groping on the banister. He watches her all the way up. She does not look back, not even when she reaches the landing and goes into the bedroom.

He opens the front door and steps out into the porch.

The rain has stopped. The black skin of the street glistens beyond the gate. He walks out and picks up a shiny purse from the grass. Inside is a tissue, a lipstick.

Back in the hall he puts the purse on the table, turns off the light, and goes slowly up the stairs.

She's already asleep. He undresses in the dark.

It is the small hours. Disturbed by a noise in the room, he sits up. The bedclothes lie empty beside him. At the end of the bed, in a cold veil of streetlight, his wife is dancing a slow, solitary waltz, one hand draped on an imaginary shoulder, the other stiffly raised, as though clasped. The floorboards are creaking under her feet. He switches on the bedside lamp. She is wearing the dress. The bedroom is filled with its damp musty smell. Her mouth is smeared red with lipstick. His skin crawls; she is asleep; she is dancing in her sleep. How eerily happy she looks, her dark dilated eyes glistening like a girl's, gazing raptly up at the face of some invisible partner waltzing her round, slowly around...

He climbs out of bed. She goes on dancing. It is only when he takes her elbows and pulls her towards him that she wakes.

Lying on the bed she begins to cry. He turns off the light and tries to take her in his arms, whispering to her. But she only stares glassily, hungrily up into the darkness above.

IN THE FOREST

Staring intently through the opera glasses, he leaned forward a fraction as the young woman on the far side of the hall settled into her seat. He watched; she turned to her neighbour, her cheeks lightly flushed, the brown little fruits of her eyes catching the light as she laughed... He slid the tip of his tongue along his lip, scarcely breathing.

'What are you looking at?' a voice muttered sharply in his ear.

He cleared his throat.

'I... thought I recognised someone.'

'Where?'

'No-one. Down in the stalls there.' He yawned and looked away, fiddling his earlobe.

His wife twisted the binoculars from his fingers and put them to her eyes, training them in the direction he'd waved too dismissively.

'Which is it?'

'Mm?' he said, feigning mild surprise that she should show any interest. He squinted. 'See the woman in the green hat? Behind her. Bald chap.'

'I don't know him.'

She began to pan along the row.

'I think we were at school...' He felt himself reddening as she paused, lingered for several seconds over some other face. (There was no need to ask oneself which.) She sniffed as if having found what she was looking for, and, wearing a little beak of distaste on her lipsticked lips, lowered the glasses and placed them fastidiously beside the programme on her lap without another word.

He sat gazing lugubriously at the proscenium.

The lights went down.

There was a sprinkling of applause as the conductor appeared and mounted the podium. With an ugly commotion of violins and cellos the orchestra embarked upon the overture.

A dull phobia began to weigh him into his seat. Why did he let himself be bullied into these evenings? Nothing bored him more than opera. She did it on purpose.

After several minutes the gold and crimson curtain floated up to reveal a forest glade. Mist drifted among the firs, beyond whose dark spires, miles away across some Tyrolean valley, a snow-draped mountain stood bathed in evening light. Centre-stage a woman in a purple dress was seated on a log. With a theatrical gesture she rose to her feet, took a few steps forward, and broke into a coloratura that would have drowned the orchestra at once had it not responded with a turgid crescendo.

He shifted his position, already restless. He was thinking of the young woman: those full lips, the way she'd lightly touched her throat when she laughed... Turning his head an inch or two, he looked across and down through the twilit fathoms to where she was sitting.

It was difficult to pick her out now the lights had dimmed. In the gloom he could hardly distinguish even her bare shoulders and arms, much less her face. Idly he imagined her sitting beside him, her slender arm carelessly touching his own... Any moment she would lean and whisper in his ear with a little giggle, slip her cool hand into his, and they'd be globed together in a sweet collusion of the dark, just he and she... He gloated secretly upon the notion, breathing softly through his nose and closing his eyes. One might have thought him captivated by the music.

The binoculars still lay on his wife's lap. He glanced down covetously. They slowly blinked, peeped slyly up at him, their lenses suddenly liquid and dark. She was holding them there like a tiny pet, lightly beating time to the music with her fingers. The glow from the stage illumined the faint hairs on her lip, her smile of cultivated appreciation. She raised her hand in an absent manner and began to stroke the loose skin of her throat, her eyelids drooping closed. The glasses lay unattended. He was just about to reach furtively across and lift them gently from her lap when her hand descended to retrieve them. The violins clambered softly. Behind the binoculars' little barrels her eyes glistened with a glue of emotion as she followed the lovers' duet in the now moonlit forest below. Stars twinkled above the trees. The music fused to a single, tremulous note; the lovers kissed, and were plunged into darkness.

The first two acts seemed interminable. When, at last, the curtain descended and the lights went up for the interval he got eagerly to his feet.

The bar was crowded. He pushed through and ordered a whiskey and a gin and tonic.

Seeing a friend from the bridge-club his wife took her drink and went across to chat. He remained standing by the bar, alone with his whiskey, alternately sipping and peering into it.

There was the usual babble all around. He couldn't understand what people found to talk about. The older he grew the less inclined he was to make the effort. More and more he found himself afflicted by that vague sense of resentment, that familiar unease with which you suspect that your life is over and done with, that the one opportunity you had of making something of it has gone; that everything in fact was long ago settled, right from the start, and that perhaps you never wanted things any other way...

Someone was laughing close behind him. It was a laugh so like his wife's – sharp and gobbled – that he couldn't help looking round.

It was the young woman.

Under the bright flat light of the bar she wasn't much to look at after all – she had a pinched sort of face, the little blob of a double chin. Yet there was something about her... He stared. It might have been his wife standing there, thirty years ago. A confused kind of longing mingled and solidified in his chest, and it was some moments before he realised that the young woman had fixed him with a stare of her own. He turned away, embarrassed, finished his whiskey in a mouthful. He looked across the foyer at his wife who was still talking.

The bell rang for the end of the intermission. People were beginning to drift towards the broad main staircase. His wife came over. She picked a bit of fluff from his shoulder, gossiping about her friend's husband who had been promoted... He wasn't listening.

As they took their seats he glanced down into the stalls. The young woman was already back in her place. He stared dully. The lights dimmed; the curtain rose. Beside him his wife had raised the opera glasses to her face. A sudden loneliness swung through him. Reaching over, he took her hand clumsily in his. She stiffened slightly, pretending not to notice, and he let go at once. He closed his eyes, feeling old and ugly and alone, and saw the tall grey forest of the years standing all around him, the grey dead forest that seemed, almost as each day passed now, to creep a little closer, to grow deeper, quieter, ever more empty.

SKYLIGHT

Life shrank to a corner of the day-room: a chair, a spindly table, flowers leaning from a vase as though even they wished quietly to observe her. Each morning when her husband came she felt she hardly knew him. He would sit on the edge of his chair, leaning forward, gently trying to engage her in conversation as she stared through the low window at the buildings opposite, where that morning the walls had sprouted hair, lank grey curls of it hanging in the rain, or the brickwork had split with shiny cysts. When she spoke it was only to tell him of these things, or of the smell, or how cold she was ... Sometimes he'd arrive to find her huddled in a blanket. Couldn't he feel the draught? she would whisper. He'd hold her hand, stroking her pale fingers with his thumb. Invariably the woman in the next chair would lean with a watery gaze, her head wobbling like some grey-bewigged doll's, and complain yet again of the enormous thrush that guarded the ward, and how it kept them awake all night with its wickety song.

In the mornings she was supposed to talk to the therapist in a room at the end of a long corridor. He would sit with his clear grey listening eyes. In the quiet afternoons she'd lie on her bed in the ward, her head crawling with strange memories, some that seemed not even hers...

Then, as suddenly as they had started, the hallucinations ceased. She sensed something inside her retreat, as if seeking some deeper, less accessible refuge.

Within another week she was discharged.

There were appointments to attend, drugs to be taken (the same white bitter little pills as before). She felt herself being eased back into her life. It frightened her. She had not wanted to go home. Something was there, undisturbed, waiting to creep into her all over again.

Her husband had been given two weeks' compassionate leave. Although it was already October he suggested they take a short holiday; in the south perhaps – France, Italy – it would do her good. The clinic advised them to wait a little longer, but she welcomed the chance to get away from the house and the oppressive solicitudes of her sister-in-law, and a few days later they left.

Crossing the Channel, the wind in her face, the sky a bright blue-and-white-painted bowl overhead, she felt alive, almost happy. She slipped her arm through her husband's, and for the first time in many weeks, in what seemed like years in fact, she laughed, gulping the cold air. They watched the dark-muscled sea sprouting clots of snowy foam at the stern below, the chalk cliffs dwindling to a smudge on the horizon. For a few hours everything seemed forgotten, left far behind...

On the night-train south she slept deeply and dreamlessly, and did not wake until they arrived in Marseilles early the following morning. From there, after breakfast in the station restaurant, they drove down to Nice.

They passed the afternoon in the old quarter of the town, walking the elegant squares and gardens, taking a stroll up and back along the Promenade des Anglais, the turquoise sea listlessly spending the last white waves of the season on the grey-pebbled beach. Sitting at a café they watched a market being dismantled, the broad street hosed down. Warm sunlight leapt from the puddles, quivering over the old pink facades and faded shutters.

By the time they set off along the route he'd planned, the day had cooled sufficiently for a pleasant drive. They took the coastal road east, the sun sinking low behind them. The sea lay glimmering like a dark blue silk, the roadside pines brushed and shining in the evening breeze.

They turned inland. She grew quiet.

It was late when they drove into the village. The mountains had withdrawn to be alone with the darkness. Sombre shapes stooped around the valley. She peered out of the car window. The moon was a tiny creature up there, a cold little embryo...

The village square was deserted. A lamp had stretched the shadow of a tree on the cobbles outside the single hotel. Somewhere a dog barked.

Behind the desk of the lobby inside, a woman was watching television. She scarcely acknowledged their arrival. Had they made a reservation? No? Turning sullenly from the flickering screen she reached behind her for a key. It was the only room available: number fourteen, on the top floor.

For two hundred and seventy francs a night the room was shabby and small, but it was too late to start looking for anything better. He dumped their cases by the wardrobe, breathing hard from having climbed four flights.

It was an attic room. The ceiling sloped claustrophobically, dangling a bare bulb. She sat on the bed, stroking the threadbare counterpane with her fingers and glancing round. Her gaze hesitated dully on a discoloured wash-basin standing in one corner. On the wall opposite the bed, above a dressing-table, hung a large ornate mirror framed with an ugly frieze of gold-painted grapes and leaves. She looked at her reflection, lifting her hand absently to her face as though it were not she but some other sitting in there.

'It's only for one night,' said her husband.

She opened her case and took out a towel, a nightie.

'We won't stay,' he murmured.

She went over to the basin in the corner and turned on the tap, holding her finger in the flutter of water. A stale breath of steam began to rise. She did not fill the stained bowl; rather she stooped, and with cupped hands splashed her face directly from the tap.

Her husband went to look for a toilet.

She whispered to herself, turning down the bedclothes, finding the sheets white and fresh. It was not a bad little room really... She plumped up the bolster, neatly laid out her husband's towel, pyjamas and washbag.

Early the next morning, venturing out to see if he could buy a paper, her husband was surprised by the peaceful spa-like atmosphere of the place. The morning was sunny and fresh, the mountains so sharp against the vivid blue of the sky that you felt you might reach out and touch them. He strolled round the narrow cobbled streets, breathing the clean air.

At breakfast he suggested they spent the day there. In fact, why not even another night? It was an interesting spot; there was a tiny cathedral, shops, a museum; she'd like it. In the afternoon perhaps, if it stayed fine, they could go for a drive.

They looked in vain however for another hotel. They could find only a dilapidated auberge. He persuaded her they might as well stay where they were; it would only be for one more night.

After lunch they took the car and followed a lane out into the terraced fields beyond. Winding back and forth it carried them up the steepening hillside. Olive groves grew either side, the trunks like twists of stone, the leaves a sage and silvery green in the afternoon light. Weeds littered the dusty ground beneath, bleached by weeks of sun.

They stopped to look down at the village: it was in fact quite large, almost a small town, meandering along the valley in a clutter of clay-coloured rooftops like a model below. The faint sounds of a provincial afternoon came floating up on the warm quiet air.

They were still some way from the top when the road abruptly narrowed to a track. He wanted to continue on foot, and she didn't argue. After twenty minutes or so, emerging onto a small outcrop, they were rewarded with a view of the Alps to the north, cloaked in bright cloud and plum-blue shadows.

They sat down on a rock, regaining their breath. The air was scented with thyme and warm resin, the only sound a thin whisper of wind in the dry shrubs and grass. A lizard appeared, observed them with the tiny glass of its eye, and then vanished. One could hear its little feet and belly rustle over the rock as it scurried away.

'You can see the sea,' he murmured. Between two hills to the south, misty in the sun, lay the pastel smudge of the Mediterranean. Then he noticed she was bent forward slightly, tensed, her arms folded across her as if she was cold. Perhaps, too, he recognised a certain look in her face.

She undressed. Her husband had gone down to check the car for the journey in the morning.

She stood looking at herself in the large mirror, and put her hand to her breasts. She ran her fingers down to the spider-dark hair between her thighs; then she slipped the nightie over her head and climbed into bed, drawing the cold sheet up to her chin with a shiver and keeping quite still to get warm.

She lay staring up, listening.

The hotel seemed inexplicably quiet. It was as though the whole building stood locked and deserted below, and she, high in the attic, was the only guest. She found her gaze resting on the skylight above. A strand of grey cobweb hung down, waving softly in some tiny draught. The frame looked half rotten, the lower sill stained brown where rain had leaked in and rusted the latch. The longer she looked the more decayed it appeared. She could not understand how she had failed to notice it as soon as they'd arrived. And there was something else; something concealed in the black oblique pane... Feeling the faint draught sinking over her face, she drew her gaze aside.

Her husband came in.

Didn't he think it was quiet? she said, as he stood at the basin brushing his teeth. He shrugged, lathering the white paste between his lips. He spat into the basin. It was late, he said. He turned, and saw her staring at the skylight.

He went over and sat down on the bed. He stroked her cheek with the back of his finger, looking into her eyes. 'Do you want to go home? We can go home tomorrow if you like. I said.'

She shook her head.

'I'll phone the clinic in the morning,' he persisted softly. 'We can make an appointment for as soon as we get back.'

'No...'

He looked at her, as though waiting for her to change her mind. She was biting the quick of her thumb. She dropped her hand. 'I'll be all right.'

He made to brush her hair gently from her forehead. She frowned and pushed his hand away.

'Did you take your tablet?' he said.

She nodded.

He went to hang his jacket in the wardrobe, and then cursed under his breath. 'I've left my wallet in the car.'

'Don't go down again,' she said, in a still voice.

'I won't be long.' He was already at the door.

No sooner had his footsteps faded on the stairs than that thick ominous silence reinhabited the room.

Suddenly she understood. Everything was clear. All those weeks she was in hospital this little attic had been waiting, like an ante-room, quietly prepared, everything in place: the mirror, the skylight, the pink faded drapes. No-one had slept here; the freshly made bed was for her alone; and now she had come, and the room was crawling silently into her, every little detail stealing a morsel of her just for itself, even the shadows, all the grey webs and sticks of them, each as though painted in thin grey oils, quietly feeding, creeping into her... The room glittered. It was alive. She saw her hand lying bloated and ugly on the blanket. She wanted it to crawl off, hide itself from sight. She looked at the large mirror beyond. The woman in there, in that other room, that other bed, was gazing melancholically out at her. A faint disgusting smell seemed to be leaking through. A carving on the wardrobe yawned, bared sharp little teeth in a libidinous grin. She shut her eyes tight, trying to squeeze it all from her head, willing her husband to return. Almost at once there came a creak.

But it was not from the staircase below.

It was from above.

A bump. A scrabble. Then another, louder bump, and as she listened, as she lay tensed and horrified, the sounds sluggishly organised themselves, became something hauling itself up the roof overhead – a slow, ponderous slithering of hands, limbs, on the tiles. Lying rigid on her back, wide-eyed, she stared up at the dark skylight where the blur of a face had appeared, fingers splayed against the dusty glass. She opened her mouth as if to scream – then, in bewilderment, sat up and whispered her husband's name. It was his face she saw at the pane, mouthing to her. She clambered from the bed, pulled the chair under the skylight. She stepped onto its lap. Standing up, she could easily reach the latch. The face was close, motionless now, looking in.

*

He locked the car and walked back over the cobbles to the hotel. He was softly admonishing himself. They shouldn't have come; he should never have suggested it...

By the time he reached the top of the stairs he'd made up his mind that they would start home first thing in the morning. He'd phone the clinic before they left. With luck they'd be home by the following evening. He opened the door to the room.

He stared at the empty bed, the bedclothes pushed back.

'Caroline?'

He went over to pick up the chair lying toppled on its back in the middle of the floor. Only then did he feel the dank draught sinking endlessly in from above. He looked up. The skylight was gaping open, the black disturbed void of the night swarming beyond.

'Caroline?'

The mirror leaned.

A JOURNEY

Within a week, and against all advice, the anthropologist embarks on a lengthy trip abroad. He flies to Corsica, and from there makes his way slowly east, to Sardinia, Sicily, then on into Calabria, staying a few days here, a week there, taking up long-standing invitations from acquaintances and former colleagues, visiting old haunts... In the second week of October he arrives in Greece, and after two nights in a stifling hotel in Athens travels out into his wife's beloved Aegean.

It has been a desolate trip, but not in the way that he expected. Perhaps he hoped it would release him from the sense of guilt and failure he feels at having discovered that there were things, ultimately, even after forty-odd years together, which she was unable to share, or more painfully simply did not want to; that just when one might have expected they would grow closer at last, something remained irrevocably between. (In those final weeks before she was admitted to the hospice she seemed selfishly to withdraw, as if all she wanted was to be left in peace with her cold little bottle of morphine, as if that was all that was left of what had once been a marriage – a few cold millilitres in a dark little bottle.) But it is not this so much that oppresses him, as the experience of finding himself suddenly alone. He never imagined. A part of him he hardly knew was there has collapsed, vanished into some motionless abyss. He feels lost. For the first time since his youth he has no-one to consider but himself, and everything he does seems utterly without meaning or purpose...

He stands alone at the rail as the third ferry in as many days carries him out into the twilight. When he and his wife made this trip eighteen months ago it was spring; the days were fresh; the sea sharp and blue, tipped with white crests. Now, on a warm October evening, there is barely a swell, and the unbreaking waves come silently flapping under the prow, black and smooth like ribbons, until the boat seems poised, as in a darkening mirror.

There are few passengers; the ferry is all but deserted, and the anthropologist remains alone on the deck for several minutes before anyone else appears – a woman comes out of the cabin, lights a cigarette. She strolls around for a while, and then joins him at the rail:

'Greece is so beautiful. In Holland we have little that is beautiful.'

Her face is lit by the light of the cabin. She is fiftyish, thin, her hair swept back, brittle and greying. A small pendant gleams at her throat. Evidently she feels obliged to make conversation, as one does, finding oneself alone with a stranger travelling through darkness. She looks at him with a mild intelligent gaze as she speaks, now and then drawing on her cigarette. The anthropologist offers no more than an occasional response, having no desire to prolong the encounter. But the woman is undeterred; she lingers beside him at the rail, speaking easily of herself. She is visiting her son. He is a solicitor. It is five years since she has seen him. She gives a self-deprecating smile and turns her face a little, as if to let the light flatter a foolish moistness in her eye.

'And you?' she adds after a moment. 'Will you be staying long in Greece?'

Although the anthropologist realises that some morsel of himself is required, some small confidence, he does not oblige: in the anonymity of night one reveals things which one later regrets.

'A week,' he replies.

The woman lets her gaze drift to one side. She discards her cigarette into the liquid darkness below, and the anthropologist finds himself resenting her intrusion all the more. Perhaps she senses it, for after a lengthy pause in which neither speaks, she makes an excuse and returns to the cabin.

The night grows cool. From time to time other passengers emerge to walk the small deck, or lean at the rail, watching the moonlight on the water.

It is a short crossing. Within an hour the boat begins to slow. It veers, and the moon slides smoothly away across the night sky. The engine throbs, the deck juddering under the anthropologist's feet. He becomes aware of his hands gripping the wooden rail. Unexpected emotions are unravelling inside him. Perhaps it was a mistake; perhaps he should not have come.

Dimly the island appears, lying like a dark wing, pricked with sparse trembling lights. A warm breeze comes floating out over the water, bringing the scent of jasmine, oleander, the lingering smell of a day sunk into dusty hills. Everything is as he remembers, and he should not have come.

They enter the harbour. A shout and a rope are flung from the quayside. The ferry bumps home to lie gently rising and falling on the harbour water, black and invisible below. The engine is cut, a gangplank lowered, and the score or so passengers disembark into the sudden quiet. One can feel the warmth rising from the quay, the hot light stored in the concrete slabs. Beyond, the small port is furnishing the night with the rustle of palms, voices, the cheep of cicadas. Somewhere a moped putters in the warm inky distance. The anthropologist walks slowly off up the main street.

*

The taverna has not changed. The doors and windows are open wide, letting the night flow softly through. Four or five locals sit at the plastic tables, drinking and talking, smoking.

Mikis is languidly paging through a newspaper spread on the bar. The anthropologist goes over. The Greek looks up, and his face splits in delight, his lips parting in a fleshy smile. He walks round from behind the bar, slapping it with his palm, and takes the anthropologist's hand in both of his, squeezing it with affection. How long has it been? Only two years? It seems so much longer. He should have come, he should have *come*. He pats the other's shoulders fondly, still smiling. And his wife? Where is his beautiful wife?

The anthropologist explains. The Greek's face falls, and then furrows. He pushes his fingers uncertainly through his dark curls, staring at the anthropologist, the black stones of his eyes oiled with emotion. He murmurs something. He seems at a loss, shaking his head in disbelief.

They talk for a while, then, as if it contained the last fragile condolence of the world, Mikis picks up the anthropologist's case, and with his hand briefly at the other's back, ushers him through and along the passage to a room.

It is the room the anthropologist and his wife had before. The anthropologist remarks upon the fact. Mikis is embarrassed. 'You prefer if...?' he begins. But the anthropologist assures him that it is the room he would have wanted. Mikis nods doubtfully. He will tell Helen who has come, he says, and retires into the passage, pulling the door to.

The anthropologist puts down his case on the bed and opens it. He pauses, and stands motionless for a moment. He feels nothing. The room seems devoid of a single memory. All that he expected is absent. A wicker chair stands at the low-silled window, looking out at the night.

He is about to start unpacking when there comes a knock on the door.

'Helen asks... You eat with us?'

Knowing it would be ungracious to refuse, the anthropologist replies in Greek that he could wish for no better company. Mikis beams with pleasure. He stands waiting in the doorway. 'Is ready,' he states after a moment.

They go through into the taverna.

His wife greets the anthropologist quietly, taking his arm and showing him to the table. Both she and Mikis seem uncertain how to express their sympathy, as though afraid to offend or intrude. As the three of them sit down to eat, the anthropologist feels ill at ease. His two friends seem like strangers suddenly; it is as if he scarcely knows them. The leaden sense of isolation which has imprisoned him since he left London weighs more heavily than ever. He picks up his fork – and then hesitates. Several times on the trip, dining with one ex-colleague after another, he has had the same momentary sensation: that he is holding not a piece of cutlery in his fingers, but the cold little morphine bottle at his wife's bedside. (Towards the end, when she was too drugged and listless to know what she was doing, he administered it himself, day after day that unspoken look in her eyes demanding something which he did not want to acknowledge. Only in the final week did she at last agree to go into the hospice. It was a relief, and he still feels guilty for having found it so.) He cuts vigorously into the lamb on his plate and enquires after his friends' fortunes. Mikis, seeming almost relieved at the opportunity, begins to talk of their plans to expand the business. They have bought a property down by the harbour. They are going to open a bar. His brother will run it. Tourists are arriving more and more on the island. Soon the town will be prosperous. Very prosperous. He taps his palm and grins sheepishly, showing the gold-filled pearls of his teeth before lapsing into an uncomfortable silence, perhaps realising that his enthusiasm has got the better of him, and that it is not the occasion. He replenishes their glasses. An owl interpolates the night outside.

The silences grow more awkward. Once the anthropologist has briefly recounted the events of the last few months, his wife's illness, its inexorable course, it is as if there were nothing more to be said; and although the meal is protracted somewhat by Mikis occasionally leaving the table to serve a customer or to exchange a few words with a passing neighbour, it is still relatively early when the anthropologist excuses himself. He is tired, he explains. It has been a long journey. He apologizes for having brought nothing but his troubles (which Mikis at once denies, shaking his head with a mumbled reproach).

Aware that there is no purpose in prolonging his own and his friends' discomfort, the anthropologist gets to his feet. As he does so, an old man in the corner of the taverna (who, all evening, has stirred no further than to avail himself of a glass of ouzo on the table before him) lifts his grey head and looks from under the palsied lids of his eyes. Raising an unsteady hand he points at the visitor, and in loud slurred Greek starts cursing and berating him. The anthropologist stands watching in surprise. The drunken tirade continues for some seconds, and then the old man falls abruptly silent, withdrawing his hand with a jerk as if it had touched something cold or unpleasant. His stick slithers to the floor with a clatter. Staring even more fixedly, he adds something unintelligible in a hoarse whisper. Mikis is already on his way across. He grips the old man's shoulder, admonishing him angrily at some length before retrieving the stick and restoring it to him. He returns, hissing softly in his teeth, shaking his head in mortification. 'Alway he is drunk,' he says (as if the fact in itself were explanation enough). 'He bring the shame to his family, to all his whole family.' The anthropologist tries to dismiss the episode, but Mikis won't hear of it. No, it is not to be excused, he says, wagging a finger at the old man like a stubby metronome. You hear? he calls with an angry jerk of his head. Eh, Yannis? You hear me? Helen touches her husband's arm. She apologizes to the anthropologist, who wishes them both goodnight and goes out into the passage.

Lying in the teeming darkness of his room he feels the slow panic crawling into him once more. After the evening's company it seems to reoccupy him more hungrily than ever. He pushes back the bedclothes in a sweat, taking a deep breath or two, trying to keep a hold of himself as it finds that place in his chest and lies still, as if it were the one remaining reason for his existence. He listens to Helen and Mikis down the passage. They are arguing about something. A door slams. All falls quiet. He thinks of what happened in the taverna: it was as if the old man knew, as if his shaking old fingers had somehow fumbled upon that cold little morphine bottle and felt everything like some senile clairvoyant – a wife's suffering, a husband's guilt, the painful ambiguities of a failed marriage… The anthropologist finds his thoughts turning to the house standing empty in London, the weeks and months waiting for him to come home and live them. It is hard to conceive that his wife won't be there when he gets back. He wonders what possessed him to come away. He has only made things worse, postponed what will eventually have to be endured. His wife wouldn't have run away like this; she would have stayed, carefully and patiently reorganising herself. He can imagine her telling him what he should do, he can almost – He wakes with a slight jolt, feeling her bump against him, her legs colliding with his as if she had turned over beside him. She lingers somewhere close. He turns onto his side and draws up his knees like a foetus, staring into the darkness. Ever since she died it has been like this, and yet he has been unable to summon up a single clear image of her face. How is that possible, after so many years? Does one grow so accustomed? There is only a sort of invisible familiarity, this vague but pervasive disembodiment of her that has become something else…

He is on the ferry. It is moving between islands of white stone and moss. He is standing at the rail, the water sliding transparently below, green like glass. Large fish are swimming, slow and grey, beautifully mottled. Their eyes are sealed with skin. His wife is standing on the deck a little way off. She has her back to him as though gazing out across the water. He tries to go to her, but he cannot move, and looking down he sees his hands are gnarled and twisted like roots grown into the wooden rail.

Next morning he wanders down to the harbour. He sits for a while, watching the fishermen cleaning up after their night's catch. He remembers the peaceful ten days or so he and his wife spent on the island. They'd got to know the Greek couple well, and he feels sad now that things seem to have come between him and his two friends.

He leaves the quayside and starts to walk up through the town. Although it is almost the end of the season there are still a few tourists about. Here and there couples browse among the small shops and stalls, mostly elderly Scandinavians or Germans, one or two English. The sunshine has cut the white-walled street into sharp compartments of light and shade. It is hot, without a breath of air. The tattered fronds of the palms hang undisturbed.

As he crosses the square he sees the old man who accosted him in the taverna. He is sitting on a bench under a large fig tree, his stick propped beside him. The fig's heavy limbs are spread and poised above like some enormous stone squid, as if his grey drunken mind had sprouted in the night. He watches the anthropologist pass, and does not stir.

Following a lane rising from the far corner of the square, the anthropologist comes to an enclosure of lime and lemon trees. It seems familiar, and when, having passed through a small iron gate and walked up the path between the groves of dark glossy-leaved trees, he emerges onto some scrubland and sees a line of tall cypresses and the pale cinnamon hills beyond, he knows he has come the right way. He picks his way across the clearing littered with breeze blocks, lumps of concrete, blue plastic bags of rubbish. A rusted moped languishes in a ditch. The morning heat is already shimmering up from the baked earth.

The track lies just as he remembers, rising gently away into the hills. His appearance from between the trees disturbs a solitary crow.

The anthropologist begins to walk along the track, the olive-white dust pluffing at his feet, thick and soft as talc. A light breeze has sprung up, and the tips of the cypresses lean in unison with a whisper.

The track leads up past a dilapidated stone hut, the roof long fallen in, the walls baked and blown to the colour of the dust, like an abandoned oven. Under the stunted trees some copper-dark straw has been strewn, and a goat stands tethered to a stick in the shade. It looks up, chewing, its crystalline eyes catching the light. From the hillside beyond comes the faint clonking of bells where a small herd is grazing. The anthropologist pauses. It seems only yesterday that he and his wife walked up this track that stilled April evening, the early flowers in bloom all around... There are no flowers now; only here and there a dried stem dipping in the breeze. He stoops, puts his fingers to the dust. It is substanceless and cool. Suddenly she is close. He stands up.

By the time he reaches the top of the rise he has all but lost control, and is shaking with sobs. He can feel her slim cold fingers in his, her voice in his head. He stumbles up the last few yards. He remembers now: just over the ridge there was an unexpected gorge...

The wind is stronger up here, and cold, as though pouring through an invisible rent. He stands at the edge. There is only the rock beneath his feet, the blue empty spasm of the sky above. He stares down into the sheltered gorge. It is as motionless and silent as before, as if not a stone or speck of dust has been disturbed. The wind leans at his back, thunders softly in his ears. He can feel her beside him. The sun gazes steadfastly over the dry brown hills.

He turns, goes back down the track.

The wind has vanished. The goats watch him push through the glare, the dust pluffing at his feet.

That evening at the meal, the anthropologist barely speaks. As soon as they have eaten he excuses himself and retires to his room. Mikis is upset. He blames himself. They have offended him, he says. It is that old winebag Yannis last night. His wife tells him he is being foolish, he must try to understand. Imagine what it is to be left alone in one's life.

All the same, the following morning she is surprised and secretly hurt when the anthropologist tells her he will be leaving the next day. He promised to visit a friend in Athens, he explains. He had forgotten. Although it is clear that this is no more than a poor excuse, and that there is some other reason, Helen does not question him. She brings him a coffee, placing the little cup and bowl of sugar carefully before him, observing him with her dark candid gaze. He is welcome to return whenever he wishes, she says. There will always be a room for him.

The anthropologist knows he should stay, if only out of courtesy. It is an insult to decline his friends' hospitality so abruptly. But his only desire is to leave. He should never have come.

Later, he meets Mikis on his way back from the market. They stand chatting for a few moments. The anthropologist doesn't tell him that he is leaving already; he can't bring himself to. Mikis has obviously resolved to make his guest feel more welcome; he holds up a string bag stuffed with fresh vegetables and a large fish. 'This evening I cook,' he says. 'Special. Special dish.' He kisses his plump lips with his fingers and grins.

The anthropologist spends the rest of the day wandering round the town, feeling ashamed. He goes to the Roman ruins, sits among the silent columns. The afternoon, hot and still under heavy cloud, fills with the tiny expressionless screams of the cicadas.

It is a subdued evening he passes with his two friends when he finally returns to the taverna. Mikis, having learnt of the anthropologist's unexpected plans, nurses a morose silence, much to his wife's annoyance.

That night the anthropologist can't sleep. He lies on top of the sheets, sweating in the stifling heat. The darkness swarms over him. Suffocated he gets up and goes to the window, opens the shutters. He sits in the wicker chair, looking out into the thick oppressive night.

Early the next morning a thunderstorm breaks, and for half an hour the little town is enclosed in the silvery rush of a downpour. The palms outside the taverna twitch and stream, the rain sparking like thistles in the street and on the flat rooftops opposite. The air cools with the smell of wetted earth. For a few minutes, as he dresses, the anthropologist feels almost a sense of release, as if somewhere his life had begun afresh.

In the afternoon, under a sky washed clean and blue, Mikis accompanies the anthropologist to the harbour, insisting on carrying his case. At the quayside the anthropologist grasps him briefly by the hand, expresses a few inadequate words of apology, and then picks up his luggage and goes up the gangplank.

The storm has brought a change of season. The Greek stands on the quay and watches the ferry bullying its way out into the cold wind and the hard dark-blue running sea. Not until it disappears beyond the headland does he turn and walk slowly back up the main street to the taverna, buttoning his jacket and looking up with a scowl as the first gust of autumn snatches at the palms.

*

The anthropologist postpones returning to England for as long as possible. The prospect of spending the winter alone in the house fills him with apprehension. He goes instead to Italy, spends a few days in Taranto, and then travels north to a cousin in Rome, with whom, although increasingly aware that he is outstaying his welcome, he lingers for a further two weeks.

It is mid-November before he eventually flies home to London.

The house is cold as a morgue. He steps over the shoal of letters obliterating the mat inside, shuts the door on the chirruping sunlight and puts down his case. He stands in the panelled hall, listening. He has been away for two months, and yet nothing has changed. All is exactly as he left it that warm September afternoon. His wife's coat is still hanging on the stand by the mirror as if she has just come in from work. Everything is quiet. He goes into the dining-room and stands at the window, looking out at the garden. A late rose is reaching up, white, drinking the light.

The days accumulate like empty boxes for which the anthropologist has no use. He drifts from one half-hearted diversion to another, trying to occupy himself. He takes out the article he was writing in the summer, only to abandon it after a single morning. He spends the weekend in the garden, raking up the dark sodden leaves, weeding, ferociously cutting things back. He even visits the university to see if the faculty might re-employ him part-time as a tutor. The secretary says she will make enquiries. Within a day or two he receives a coolly apologetic letter from the proctor's office.

For a while he endeavours to spend the evenings out, visiting friends, relatives, even taking himself to the theatre again. But to return each time to the empty house becomes so intolerable that he soon reverts to the habit of staying in, eating a solitary supper in the kitchen, and spending the rest of the evening in his study upstairs. Sometimes he can hear himself still moving about in the quiet rooms below; or there is a whispering, like a soft breeze down there...

The weeks merge. It is not until one afternoon in February, going through his wife's wardrobe, sorting out her clothes at last, that the anthropologist realises what he is going to do, and that he has known all along, ever since he returned.

After supper he sits down at his desk and writes to Mikis and Helen. He asks them to find him a small flat to rent for the spring and summer. He is coming back... And even as he writes, sitting in the musty silence of the study, the night at the window, the trees imprisoned in the darkness beyond, he can feel the warm Aegean air in his lungs, the sunlight on his face. He closes his eyes, remembering the plans he'd made when he and his wife were there. Yes, he'll go back, live quietly in the little town for a while, explore the islands, write that book he has been promising himself for the last three years. Perhaps he'll stay. Why not? Perhaps he'll – He opens his eyes, sits motionless. He gets to his feet.

Outside the study he stands listening. There isn't a sound. He walks along the landing, stops, listens again. The house is as quiet as ever, and yet... Suddenly he is aware of the cypresses, tall like a line of shadows behind him. The track is quietly waiting. He can feel the dust, cool and soft in his fingers... And then he is standing up there on the edge of the gorge, the rock beneath his feet, the wind pushing at his back, and he sways forward in the darkness at the top of the stairs, gripping the banister.

ACKNOWLEDGEMENTS

Ruth Sharman
The *Sunday Times, The Observer, The Independent, London Magazine, Poetry Review, The Faber Book of Murder* (1994). Prizes: Arvon International Poetry Competition (*Birth of the Owl Butterflies*); Canterbury Festival Poetry Competition (*Knife*).

Alison Spritzler-Rose
Home Movies won second prize in the 1997 Kensington & Chelsea Arts Council competition, *Anatomy* was published in the Erotic Print Society Review and *Cherries* appears in an illustrated limited pamphlet by Clarion Press.

Catherine Conzato
The Severed Reef was published in *Antipodes*, the North American Journal of Australian Literature, June 1995. *The Egg Run* was published in *Antipodes*, June 1996.

The stories by **John Gower** in *Two Plus Two* are previously unpublished.

Staple First Editions

David Lightfoot	LAST ROUND	1991
Jennifer Olds	THE HALF-ACRE RANCH	1992
Peter Cash	FEN POEMS	1992
Adrienne Brady Ted Burford John Latham Paul Munden David Winwood	QUINTET	1993
Donna Hilbert	WOMEN WHO MAKE MONEY AND THE MEN WHO LOVE THEM	1994
Jennifer Olds	AN EXTRA HALF-ACRE	1995
Julia Casterton Tobias Hill Joan Jobe Smith Huw Watkins Howard Wright Alicia Yerburgh	SESTET	1995
Gregory Warren Wilson	PRESERVING LEMONS	1996
Ruth Sharman Alison Spritzler-Rose Catherine Conzato John Gower	TWO + TWO	1997

Staple
and
Staple First Editions

Staple New Writing, established 1982, is published in March July and December of each year. Though Staple magazine has an entirely open policy, the collections series Staple First Editions can only consider work which meets the published conditions.